Praise for S

I worry about many parenting narratives ar ve they are harmful to the kids of this generation. When I read this book, my overarching response was "Thank You." Finally someone is talking about what truly helps children thrive. Finally someone is talking about equipping kids for life. Thank you, Jill, for giving parents not a new theory, but a new reminder of how people are actually designed to function, and a guide to helping children grow into that kind of person.

DR. HENRY CLOUD, psychologist and *New York Times* bestselling author

Jill Garner masterfully combines biblical wisdom, hard lessons learned from our nation's mistaken preoccupation with self-esteem, illuminating research on effective parenting, inspiring stories from real families, and insights from her lifetime of leadership in "heart-centered" character education to teach us the ingredients of parenting that are needed to develop a "StrongHeart"—a morally courageous young person grounded in truth and able to withstand the temptations of the world to become all God created them to be. In a culture struggling to regain its moral and spiritual compass, what could be more important?

DR. THOMAS LICKONA, PhD, developmental psychologist, author of *How to Raise Kind Kids* and *Character Matters*

Parents are desperate, and this book fills a deep need. In this social media culture, our children are being overwhelmed with twisted images and warped values. The pressure to conform to insane ideologies is greater than ever before. With flaming arrows being fired at their kids from every conceivable angle, parents often feel helpless. In *StrongHeart*, Jill Garner says, "Not so fast. You are not powerless!" Then, with *hope* and *practicality*, she offers the methods and strategies from a biblical perspective to raise, as she says, "children insulated from the lies of our culture without being isolated from the world—children who become StrongHearts that lead their generation in the right direction." It's not too late to empower our children to impact the culture for good. Read this book to find out why.

DR. TIM CLINTON, author, and president of the American Association of Christian Counselors

StrongHeart emphasizes the importance of nurturing and protecting the hearts of children from negative influences in society while also preparing them to navigate the world with a strong foundation in their beliefs and values. By instilling a biblical worldview, this book aims to provide children with a solid moral compass to help them withstand the challenges they may encounter in a world filled with negative influences. The qualities of "guts, resilience, integrity, and tenacity" are just a few of the many essential attributes to develop. Jill offers valuable insights and practical guidance to raise children who are grounded in their beliefs, resilient in the face of adversity, and equipped to make positive choices in an increasingly evil world.

LEE ANN MANCINI, author of *Raising Kids to Follow Christ: Instilling a Lifelong Trust in God*; founder of Raising Christian Kids; author and executive producer of the Sea Kids series

I've known Jill and have been a fan of her ministry and teaching for many years. This book may be one of her best. Borne from much experience and wisdom, *StrongHeart* will help parents in their endeavor to raise children who are mentally, emotionally, relationally, and spiritually healthy. I found myself nodding in agreement often as I read. Jill's thought that modern parents usually opt to entertain their children rather than train them, to be their cheerleader rather than their coach, their sidekick instead of their shepherd, is worthy of study. This book can help you avoid many dangerous parent traps. Read it, study, and apply it. You'll not regret having done so.

DR. WALT LARIMORE, MD, internationally recognized family physician educator and award-winning, bestselling author

Are you on a quest to be the best parent you can be? Do you want to raise your child to do the right thing for the right reason? Then read *StrongHeart*. Jill Garner's approach to character formation is grounded in biblical wisdom and her steeled belief that a child's heart can be strengthened with grit, integrity, and humility. Then, fortified with purpose and resiliency that leads to joy.

DR. ARTHUR SCHWARTZ, president, Character.org

The children are our future. That's why the enemy is after them. If there was ever a need for resilient, formidable, and excellent young men and women, it is now. In her new book, *StrongHeart*, Jill Garner empowers parents with biblically sound tools to raise children who will have the courage to stand up against the tide of darkness in the culture and then, with a spirit of humility and respect, rise to the top in those areas God places them.

MAX DAVIS, author and *New York Times* bestselling author

When children have strong hearts, they can withstand the onslaught of cultural lies and ignore people's manipulation. This means they can become who God created them to be and accomplish what they've been called to do. This book is essential now! Read it. Jill communicates her significant ideas with great clarity. For example, the lists of contrasts will make it easy for you to understand her and agree with her. But that won't satisfy you. You'll want to apply the ideas because she writes with such a compassionate force. She has given me much to think about and do, and I pray you'll be open to the insights, too.

DR. KATHY KOCH, founder of Celebrate Kids, Inc.; author of seven parenting books, including *Parent Differently* and *8 Great Smarts*

JILL GARNER

StrongHeart

Cultivating Humility, Respect, and Resiliency in Your Child

MOODY PUBLISHERS
CHICAGO

Scripture quotations marked (KJV) are from the King James Bible.

All emphasis in Scripture has been added.

Some content was previously published in the author's books *Raising Respectful Children in a Disrespectful World* and *Raising Unselfish Children in a Self-Absorbed World.*

Names and details of some stories have been changed to protect the privacy of individuals.

Published in association with the literary agency of The Steve Laube Agency, 24 W. Camelback Rd., A-635, Phoenix, AZ 85013.

Edited by Amanda Cleary Eastep
Interior design: Ragont Design
Cover design: Faceout Studio, Molly von Borstel
Cover element of red blood background copyright © 2023 by Jose A. Bernat Bacete/Getty Images (1363576325). All rights reserved.
Cover design of crystal heart copyright © 2023 by Ekaterina Glazkova/Shutterstock (566357902). All rights reserved.
Author photo: Eye Wander Photo

Library of Congress Cataloging-in-Publication Data

Names: Garner, Jill, author.
Title: Strongheart : cultivating humility, respect, and resiliency in your child / Jill Garner.
Description: Chicago : Moody Publishers, 2024. | Includes bibliographical references. | Summary: "Heart-focused, evidence-based solutions for raising brave, resilient, and kind children"-- Provided by publisher.
Identifiers: LCCN 2023058764 (print) | LCCN 2023058765 (ebook) | ISBN 9780802429070 (paperback) | ISBN 9780802473936 (ebook)
Subjects: LCSH: Parenting--Religious aspects--Christianity. | Child rearing--Religious aspects--Christianity. | BISAC: RELIGION / Christian Living / Parenting | RELIGION / Christian Living / General
Classification: LCC BV4529 .G3695 2024 (print) | LCC BV4529 (ebook) | DDC 248.8/45--dc23/eng/20240308
LC record available at https://lccn.loc.gov/2023058764
LC ebook record available at https://lccn.loc.gov/2023058765

Originally delivered by fleets of horse-drawn wagons, the affordable paperbacks from D. L. Moody's publishing house resourced the church and served everyday people. Now, after more than 125 years of publishing and ministry, Moody Publishers' mission remains the same—even if our delivery systems have changed a bit. For more information on other books (and resources) created from a biblical perspective, go to www.moodypublishers.com or write to:

Moody Publishers
820 N. LaSalle Boulevard
Chicago, IL 60610

1 3 5 7 9 10 8 6 4 2

Printed in the United States of America

Contents

Author's Note

Think of all the things parents teach their children. They teach them how to sit still, listen, keep their hands to themselves, ride a bicycle, pray, sew, cook, study, clean, do yard work, be respectful, be a lady, be a gentleman, be a good sport, love well, forgive. The list is endless.

Our role as parents is to lead and train our children with love and grace for today. God's role as Father is to save and to secure His children with love and grace for eternity. While we are reaching into our children's hearts, God is working in their hearts to stir a desire to follow Jesus. He is wooing, directing, calling, moving, and redirecting.

God called me to Himself at the age of seven. Running down the aisle of our church and jumping into the arms of our pastor remains the most vivid memory of my childhood. In that moment, I shouted out, "I want Jesus in my heart" with all the excitement and belief possible in a young child.

My mother and daddy didn't create that desire in my heart—God did. Leading up to that moment, I was tucked in bed at night. I was loved well. Chores were part of our training. Respect was nonnegotiable—respect for God's Word, respect for my parents, and respect for others. My parents kept my heart open to the good news of the gospel.

Parents have a holy duty to show their children the way they should go: it is to lead them down the path of righteousness as godly parents. Ultimately, it is God who does the deep work of changing hearts.

INTRODUCTION

Who Is a StrongHeart?

When it comes to understanding the role of the heart as it relates to brain function and decision-making, it could be that we (experts, psychologists, physicians, parents) are not as smart as fifth graders, as a once popular game show reminded us.

Let me explain . . .

I was asked to give a fifth-grade commencement address a few years ago as founder of the nonprofit Manners of the Heart, and creator of the elementary school curriculum, *HeartEd.*

The mission of my organization is to bring an awakening of respect and civility in our society by establishing Heart Education as the foundation of education in our country. The curriculum teaches children to respect and esteem others, and in the process, gain respect for themselves.

This local public school had been utilizing our program for five years, so I was confident these students fully understood that whatever they think, say, or do originates in their hearts. After much thought, I decided to rely on the students to give the foundational information for the address through a series of questions.

When I arrived at the school the morning of the commencement ceremony, a few students offered to help with the setup. We visited for a few minutes, but I kept the content of the speech they would soon hear out of our conversation. After being introduced to a filled auditorium, I moved to the floor in front of the students and opened with the statement, "You're Manners of the Heart kids, and that means you should be ready to take on middle school. We're here today to find out!"

Without further explanation, I turned to a whiteboard and drew an outline of a character I labeled StrongHeart. I then asked, "What's in the heart of a StrongHeart?"

Hands shot up across the room with one word shout-outs: "Confidence. Kindness. Self-control. Obedience. Compassion. Perseverance. Love. Forgiveness. Respect. Patience. Gratitude," and on and on.

With each answer, my smile broadened, as my heart burst with excitement.

I wrote their answers inside the heart as fast as I could. The teachers and parents were as proud of the children as I was. Many were surprised. I was amazed, but not surprised at all.

"Looks like the heart of a great kid," I exclaimed. "I would say, most definitely a StrongHeart! Soon, you will leave elementary school behind and step into the world of middle school. There will be many people, including your closest friends, who will try their hardest to break down your strong heart, who will tempt you with all kinds of offers that will seem fun in the moment."

The students were listening intently, as evidenced by their posture and eagerness to hear more. Pointing to the whiteboard, I added, "I want you to see what will happen to your heart if you give in to the temptations. Let's use the heart of our character StrongHeart as an example."

Upon my request, the students offered scenarios of how they might be tempted. Those fifth graders called out everything from sex and cheating on a test, to fighting and drugs.

"You already know the offers that will come, don't you?" I asked. "I want you to understand what takes place in your heart as you answer those invitations.

"If you say yes, when you should say no, you'll break a piece of your heart," I said, erasing a section of the heart outline. "Do it again, and you'll break another piece of your heart," I continued, erasing another piece of the heart, and then, another, until we'd made it through their scenarios. By the end of the exercise, the protective wall of StrongHeart's heart had been completely removed.

"Before you realize what's happening to you, your heart will begin to fall apart. If your heart falls apart, what happens to the good stuff that's in it?" I quizzed.

Multiple voices shouted, "Bad stuff gets in."

"That's right," I exclaimed with utter delight (for every Manners of the Heart kid learns—you take the bad stuff out and put the good stuff in, and if the good stuff falls out, the bad stuff gets back in).

As I turned back to our StrongHeart figure, I asked, "What happens to the love in StrongHeart's heart?"

The students responded, "It turns to hate."

"What happens to the respect?" I asked.

"It becomes disrespect," they answered.

When the exercise was complete, StrongHeart was left with nothing good in his heart. Anticipating answers, such as "weak, broken, mad, or sad," I asked, "Who has StrongHeart become?"

Without hesitation, a typically timid girl in the front row whispered under her breath, "Depressed."

A young man from the back shouted, "He's a murderer."

A hush fell across the room. Only sighs and deep breathing could be detected. His profound answer stunned everyone in the auditorium. The depth of his understanding was astonishing.

Other children called out, "Mean. Scary. Sad."

Now, the tough question, "Who broke the heart of StrongHeart?"

There was a long silence, until one young man bravely raised his hand and with a question in his words, said, "He did?"

"Yeah," someone said from down the row, "I did too."

"Me, too," nodded one of the girls.

"You're right," I responded. "You break your own heart when you make the wrong choices. I break my heart when I make wrong decisions. When we allow the bad stuff to take over, look what happens to us . . . we lose our hearts, and we have no one to blame but ourselves. *But* there's good news. It can be fixed. Do you know who can fix it?" I asked with a fist pump over my heart.

"StrongHeart can," said one.

"I can," said another.

"We can fix our hearts," the rest joined in agreement.

"How do we do it?" I asked.

A girl on the front row called out, "By remembering our *Manners of the Heart* lessons!"

"You're right!" I agreed with a nod.

One by one we reverted the disheartening attributes back to love, respect, kindness, forgiveness.

Pointing to our recovering StrongHeart, I explained, "The more your heart fills with the good stuff, the stronger you become. With each right choice, you put a piece of your heart back together." With each right answer, I traced the wall of StrongHeart's heart, until we had created an impenetrable barrier around the good contents within it. "After a while, your heart becomes so strong, it becomes easier to make the right choices and harder to make the wrong choices. When that happens, you and our StrongHeart become leaders others want to follow."

One of the more rambunctious boys jumped to his feet and began pounding his fist over his heart as he chanted, "I want to be a StrongHeart! I want to be a StrongHeart!" In a heartbeat, all the children joined in.

My, how utterly thunderstruck I was that day with the wisdom of the children. They proved that the heart informs the mind. They understood the attitude that determines their actions is formulated in their hearts. They demonstrated the way in which the content of their hearts determines what they think, say, and do. They accepted responsibility for the choices they make, knowing there is no one to blame but themselves for poor choices, while fully understanding how to get themselves back on track.

In this exercise, my goal was to show the children how to take accountability for their choices before they entered middle school. You can only imagine how much my heart wanted to take these precious children to the deeper level of understanding that only God can change a heart, but in our present public-school environment, I was not at liberty to offer the whole truth.

On this day, my prayer was that their hearts were being kept fertile soil for the good news of the gospel to pour in and do the work of salvation. This is not the outcome of mindfulness, meditation, or manipulation. This is the outcome of Heart Education.

Your StrongHeart child will affect the world for good rather than become infected by it.

Within the pages of this book, you'll find practical advice that will equip you to raise a StrongHeart, a morally courageous child, grounded in truth and fortified with self-respect, who is able to overcome the trials of life and resist the temptations of our culture to become all he or she is meant to be. Your StrongHeart child will affect the world for good rather than become infected by it.

You can raise your child to become a StrongHeart if you're willing to:

- Choose self-respect and forget self-esteem as your parenting goal.
- Establish your home on a foundation of respect to counteract outside influences.
- Cultivate lasting joy in your child by letting go of happiness as the end-all of life.
- Instill gratitude in your child's heart that combats their innate greediness.
- Foster humility that endears your child to others.
- Encourage bravery so your child will be able to stand when others can't.
- Develop GRIT to build your child's character.
- Practice others-centeredness to combat the world's push toward self-indulgence.
- Champion respect by striving to be the person you want your child to become.

Please don't feel overwhelmed. It's not as complicated as it may seem at this moment. Three guiding principles lay the foundation for raising a StrongHeart:

1. The content of the heart—whether good, bad, or ugly—formulates what your child will think, say, or do, which establishes the education of the heart.
2. Esteeming others develops self-respect in your child.
3. Respect for God's Word is the foundation of parenting.

There you have it. Three simple but profound truths that, if followed, will guide you through the most important endeavor of your life—**raising children insulated from the lies of our culture without being isolated from the world**—children who become StrongHearts that lead their generation in the right direction.

Thank you for the privilege of walking alongside you in your parenting journey. I will do my best to help you, for the sake of your children and their children.

To access a small group study guide,
including discussion questions and HeartWork for the Home,
visit jillgarnercontent.org/smallgroupstudy.

CHAPTER ONE

Choose Self-Respect, Forget Self-Esteem

STRONG, adj. *Having ability to bear or endure; firm; solid; as a constitution strong enough to bear the fatigues of a campaign.*[1]

My father was not a healthy man during my high school years. Medicine bottles lined the ledge over the fireplace in the living room. Each time he took a pill, he flipped the bottle upside down to maintain a daily regimen of treatment prescribed by his doctor.

Daddy listened to those in charge of his care and followed their orders as best he could. His hope was to find his way back to health, to find a way to reverse the disease attacking his ever-weakening heart to make it strong again.

I've never forgotten the day Daddy came home from the pharmacy with a fresh refill only to discover the new pills weren't the same as the previous prescription. He was "dog mad," grabbed his keys, and headed back to town to take a bite out of the person in charge.

I waited for Daddy's return. More than an hour later, he pulled in the driveway. I greeted him at the door. "Daddy, did you get the medicine straightened out?" I asked.

"Yep," he replied.

"Everything's fine now?" I asked.

"Nope," Daddy said. "When I confronted the pharmacist, he admitted I was right. There had been a mistake. The pill I had been taking for six weeks was the wrong medicine."

I was aghast.

Of all the pill bottles sitting on the mantel, the medicine Daddy needed most to control the buildup of fluid around his heart had been incorrectly dispensed. No wonder that rather than improving, his health had been deteriorating by the day.

Even though Daddy followed the advice of his doctors, someone who played a critical role in his care had made a dreadful mistake.

Two weeks later Daddy left this earth for his heavenly home.

Why do I share such a difficult story? Just as the wrong medicine dispensed to Daddy did not cure him but hurt him, we have been taking the wrong medicine to cure the ills of our society since the 1960s. Psychotherapist Nathaniel Branden adopted William James's theory of self-esteem from the late 1800s and published a seminal work in 1969 titled *The Psychology of Self-Esteem*,[2] in which he promoted the concept of loving oneself.

During the same time period, Carl Rogers, one of the founders of humanistic psychology, promoted the idea of "unconditional positive regard," a technique he intended as a means for helping kids cope with feelings of inadequacy in the eyes of their parents when they failed to meet certain goals.[3]

Both Branden and Rogers believed the answers we needed to find our way out of the tumultuous '60s would be found in the building of self-esteem.[4] I believe it was the wrong prescription that has nearly destroyed two generations and is now threatening to destroy another.

I know most of you reading this only know what you know about the '60s from what you've read or been told by parents and grandparents who lived through it. Or you're a fan of the iconic music. Or you love the vintage style of clothing and décor.

The political upheaval, rioting in the streets, lawlessness, confusion, and social unrest that characterize today were present then too. Along with the Vietnam War, Woodstock, President Kennedy's assassination, and the rise of the counterculture, the '60s were not unlike what we experience today in the 2020s—with one grand exception.

In the '60s, the self-esteem movement was in its infancy, accepted as a solution to the troubles of that decade's young people. Today, it is widely viewed as an essential component of mental health.[5] The truth that self-esteem was introduced to our society in the late 1800s by psychiatrist William James as a theory of human development has been forgotten.

Let's look at the results of this thinking.

Self-Esteem as the "Cure"

It's true. Parents who were Baby Boomers themselves did what they were told. By the late 1970s, many Boomer parents had bought into the self-esteem movement and began smothering their children with attention. Lavishing gifts for every A and praising children for even small achievements became commonplace. Most of all, making sure their children were happy, first and foremost, was established as the new goal of successful parenting.

As a Baby Boomer parent myself, I can testify that many of us entertained our children without training them. We took care of their lives, so our children didn't learn to take care of themselves. I have often said we didn't help our children develop two legs to stand on, so too many have needed crutches to stand.

Frank Stephenson, cultural analyst, noted, "By 1985, a tidal wave of self-esteem awareness was breaking over nearly every cultural beachhead in the land. Suddenly, the 'me' generation was in full swing, swaying to the mantra of self-worth at any cost."[6]

Parents of the 1980s did all of this so their children would feel special. As the self-esteem movement continued to take hold into the '90s,[7] every kid got a trophy or a ribbon or a citation or a something just for standing where they were told, but even the children could sense the fraudulence. After an end-of-the-year baseball party for a team of ten-year-olds, one of my sons jumped in the backseat and threw his trophy on the floorboard. When I suggested he should be appreciative of his award, he retorted, "Mom, I don't deserve a trophy. I didn't do anything but stand out there. I don't want it."

Worst of all, while more and more parents became obsessed with making their children feel special, with society supporting their obsession, they were failing to ground their children in truth.

In the '90s, relativism was allowed to sneak in under the guise of building children's self-esteem because it's hard to teach truth when you're caught up in a lie. How do you find time to teach Proverbs when you're busy making sure your child will have the right activities on their college application?

How do you teach children to cooperate with each other when you're worried about your child beating out the other kids in their grade for the best scholarship?

The character Dash from Pixar's *Incredibles* film drives home this point when he gets in trouble at school for using his superpowers to play pranks on his teacher. On the car ride home, Dash defends himself to his mother by saying, "Our powers make us special," to which his mom, Mrs. Incredible, responds, "Everyone is special, Dash." Dash snaps back, "Which is another way of saying that no one is."[8]

Now, the Millennials, the first generation of self-esteem-filled adults, are raising Gen Z and Gen Alpha.* They're filling the days of their children with activities, classes, and lessons. Toddlers are enrolled in tumbling, dance, gymnastics, and soccer. The entertainment of children has risen to a new level. There's music, lights, and action in every minute of every day. Children are responding with over-the-top behavior from the overstimulation of their surroundings. (We'll talk more about this and the following topics in upcoming chapters.)

It's not all bad. Dads are more involved in the lives of their children than ever before. They're at games, going to doctor's appointments, and playing in the backyard, which are good things. But entertainment that's not balanced with training won't meet the heart needs of children.

Let's take a fresh look at an often-quoted Scripture in Proverbs, "Train a child up in the way he should go: and when he is old, he will not depart from it" (Prov. 22:6 KJV). In the original text, "train" is *chanak*, which means to discipline, dedicate, or inaugurate.[9] The word used for way is *derek*, which means a course for life, road, or journey.[10] To train your child means to equip them for their course in life. To help them find God's purpose for their life.

With all the best intentions of the Boomers, Gen X and Millennials—and subsequent generations—are struggling in ways that could have been avoided. The pursuit of self-esteem led parents to pacify their children, to be more concerned with keeping their children happy than helping their children mature. Because parents gave them all the world had to offer, many became addicted to the world's offerings, finding that fame, fortune, and fun do not ultimately bring fulfillment, only emptiness. Rather than helping children develop strong hearts, too often our society witnesses young hearts broken into pieces.

* To find a detailed description of the generations, as outlined in this book, visit jillgarnercontent.org/generations.

In some ways this was a predictable surprise. Prioritizing anything over the truth found in God's Word will bring struggles. The tenets of the self-esteem movement are not found in Scripture but in the writings of man. We lost sight of the truth that self-esteem was the culprit not the cure for our ills. Statistics reflect the impact of decades of following the prescription for building self-esteem:

- At least one in five youth aged nine to seventeen years currently has a diagnosable mental health disorder that causes some degree of impairment; one in ten has a disorder that causes significant impairment.[11]
- Between 1999 and 2019, there was a 64 percent increase in the use of antidepressants.[12]
- The most common mental illnesses in adolescents are anxiety, mood, attention, and behavior disorders.[13]
- Suicide is the second leading cause of death in young people aged ten to twenty-four years.[14]
- In 2022, over three-quarters of college students (77 percent) experienced moderate to serious psychological distress.[15]
- Thirty-five percent of college students were diagnosed with anxiety.[16]
- Twenty-seven percent of college students were diagnosed with depression.[17]

In the last sixty years, we have swallowed massive doses of self-esteem, and in turn given it to our children. Just as the medicine given to Daddy made his heart weaker, this incorrect diagnosis has made us weaker as individuals and as a society.

The esteeming of self is contrary to the teaching of Scripture, which teaches us to esteem God and to esteem others. The adoption of self-esteem is the root cause of our struggles.

Jennifer Crocker, psychologist at the University of Michigan's Institute for Social Research, explains further: "Self-esteem has short-term benefits but long-term costs, ultimately diverting people from fulfilling their fundamental human needs for competence, relatedness and autonomy, leading to poor self-regulation and mental and physical health."[18]

Take a look at my "Ten Commandments of 'Self-Esteemism'":

1. You shall have no other gods before You.
2. You shall make for Yourself idols in the form of anything in heaven above or on earth beneath.
3. You shall misuse the name of the lord Your god and hold anyone guiltless who misuses his name.
4. Remember this day by keeping it happy.
5. Dishonor Your father and your mother, so You may live long in the land You give Yourself.
6. You shall not murder unless the Supreme Court declares it justified.
7. You shall have sex in the city, sex in the country, sex anywhere You desire.
8. You shall not steal unless You must possess what You cannot afford.
9. You shall give false testimony against Your neighbor to improve Your feelings of worth.
10. You shall covet Your neighbor's house until You build a house they shall covet.

I mean no disrespect or irreverence of God's Word by this list. Quite the contrary. I hope this shows that self-esteem is the antithesis of scriptural teaching. Unless we abandon the false teaching of self-esteem, another generation—your children's generation—will suffer even greater harm.

If Not Self-Esteem, Then What?

Children don't need self-esteem, they need self-respect. Clear and simple. We were not wired to esteem ourselves. When we raise children to esteem themselves, they short-circuit. Their decision-making process is disjointed and becomes disconnected from reality. They make decisions based in what feels good in the moment rather than what *is* good.

Self-esteem and self-respect can seem synonymous to many. So, let me offer a word picture that I use in parent workshops to clear the fog between self-esteem and self-respect:

> It's Saturday night. Two sixteen-year-old girls, independent of each other, are on a date. Sue is filled with self-esteem. Sarah is filled with self-respect.
>
> It's getting late. The movie is over. Friends are gone. The girls are alone with their dates. Each of them receives a proposition. Which girl will make the best decision? Sarah, full of self-respect, or Sue, full of self-esteem?
>
> The answer: Sarah, full of self-respect. (I bet you're nodding your head.)
>
> With little thought and much confidence, Sarah tells her date it's time to go home. He persists. She insists. Sarah stands her ground. He takes her home. End of story.
>
> Sue reluctantly agrees to her date's request because, in the moment, she craves his attention more than she desires to maintain her dignity. For Sue, this is just the beginning of her story.
>
> Monday morning rolls around. The two girls step onto the campus of their high school. Sarah speaks to everyone and asks what they did over the weekend. Sue has a hard time making eye contact. She's wondering who knows what she did.
>
> The inevitable reframing of her self-image begins.

We know now where Sue's self-esteem came from, but where did Sarah's self-respect come from? What did she understand about herself that Sue did not understand? What was the difference in how they were being parented that led to these two drastically different outcomes?

No doubt, Sue's parents believed self-esteem would give their daughter confidence to make good decisions, but those who told Sue's parents to build her self-esteem were wrong. Sue had to have all the attention, even when it was the wrong attention. Sarah's parents, on the other hand, held to an old-fashioned, but not antiquated, parenting philosophy of teaching their daughter to esteem others, which, in the process, developed her self-respect.

Self-Respect as the Real Cure

I'm often challenged by others that self-respect is still a focus on self, but in reality, it's a focus on others. Let me explain.

To open a parenting workshop on the topic of respect, I pose the question, "How do you gain respect?" The most common answers are:

By giving it
By earning it
By expecting it
By demanding it

If I ask you the same question, I suspect your answer would fall somewhere on this list. It is true: to get respect, you must give respect. Respect is gained by esteeming others. Respect cannot be demanded; instead, it is commanded by your attitude, choices, and treatment of others.

Self-esteem and self-respect are not synonyms, but polar opposites. The difference between self-esteem and self-respect is best understood using a mirror and a window for illustration.

Imagine standing in front of a group of friends, holding a mirror in front of your face. As you gaze in the mirror, you only see yourself. You cannot see others in the room through the mirror. You cannot see others looking at you.

When we seek to build our children's self-esteem, we place a mirror in their hands and say, "It's all about you. What you feel and what you want." But we know the longer we gaze into a mirror, the worse things look, don't we? The same is true for children. The longer your child lives in the mirror, the more lost they become in themselves, becoming either self-conceited or self-conscious.

When we put the mirrors down and take children to a window, they see their own reflection, but it's against the backdrop of the world. At the window of self-respect, they catch of glimpse of themselves, but they immediately see past themselves, beyond themselves to the world before them. (We'll dive deeply into raising children in the mirror or at the window in chapter 8.)

David Brooks, a journalist with the *New York Times* and author of *The Road to Character*, describes his realization concerning the need to abandon a philosophy focused on the esteeming of self, and return to the cultivation of self-respect. Brooks writes:

> People with character may be loud or quiet, but they do tend to have a certain level of self-respect. Self-respect is not the same as self-confidence or self-esteem. Self-respect is not based on IQ or any of the mental or physical gifts that help get you into a competitive college. It is not comparative. It is not earned by being better than other people at something. It is earned by being better than you used to be, by being dependable in times of testing, straight in times of temptation. It emerges in one who is morally dependable. Self-respect is produced by inner triumphs, not external ones. It can only be earned by a person who has endured some internal temptation,

who has confronted their own weaknesses and who knows, "Well, if worse comes to worst, I can endure that. I can overcome that."[19]

If you choose to build self-respect in your children, you'll focus on who your kids are becoming rather than what they will do.

If you choose to build self-respect in your children, you'll focus on who your kids are becoming rather than what they will do. You'll teach them how to serve others rather than waiting to be served. You'll teach your kids to do their best while working toward goals so they can experience the satisfaction and confidence that a job well done brings.

Which Will You Choose?

For more than fifty years, we have sought after, worked toward, and obsessed over self-esteem in the development of children. It has become obvious that this approach has not worked in the home, in the classroom, or in our society.

You have a choice to make in raising your children or impacting the children you serve in your sphere of influence. Will you choose self-esteem or self-respect as your goal? Let's look at the distinct differences between the outcomes of pursuing the development of self-esteem and self-respect:

Self-esteem	**Self-respect**
Fleeting happiness	Lasting joy
Greediness	Gratefulness
Arrogance	Humility
Insecurity	Confidence
Seeking approval	Approved
Wanting more	Having enough
Self-serving	Self-giving

Self-esteem cont.	**Self-respect cont.**
Gives up	Resilient
Fearful	Brave
Self-centered	Others-centered
Self-exaltation	Self-forgetfulness
Artificial	Authentic

We were told if we focused on self-esteem, our children would exude all the qualities in the righthand column. Seems we were duped into believing a lie. Let's take a closer look.

Fleeting Happiness or Lasting Joy

Imagine standing with your child at a crossroads. Looking ahead to the left is a sign with an arrow that reads, "Self-esteem this way." On the path to the right, a sign with an arrow pointing in the opposite direction reads, "Self-respect this way." Just ahead, there is a sharp turn in each path. You can't see where the paths lead.

Looking behind you, you see only a dark forest. No path or opening in the dense plantings. It is obvious that the only option you have is to move forward with your child. The decision to be made is: Which path will you take? There is no path up the middle.

The quest for self-esteem will take your child down a path toward destruction. The quest for self-respect will take your child down a path toward humility, wisdom, and salvation in Christ. My hope is that you will make the right choice for the sake of your child(ren).

Will you choose happiness or joy for your children? Your child experiences something far beyond happiness when he or she discovers their talents and realizes the satisfaction of contributing value to our society. Joy is found in becoming who you were meant to be.

Greediness or Gratefulness

I know what I'm about to share is contrary to what most child experts say, but it is true. Your child was born with a greedy heart. Your toddler didn't *learn* to say, "It's mine," or "I had it first." Both phrases came out of your child's inward-focused heart.

Nicholaus Noles, a developmental psychologist at the University of Louisville, designed a series of studies for two- and three-year-olds who were shown identical toys and told that one was theirs and the other was not. In the first study, the children kept their eye on their own toy when the toys were shuffled. In a second study, the children were asked which toy they liked best, even though the toys were identical. With rare exceptions, the children said they liked "theirs" the best. In a third study, they were shown a block of wood and told it was theirs. An amazing number of children said they liked the block of wood better than the toy that belonged to someone else. They chose a wood block labeled as theirs over a toy that was not.

When questioned why the children would choose as they did, Noles commented, "That's just the way we're wired."[20]

He is right. The wiring runs from the heart to the frontal cortex, not the other way around. In support of this belief, research from John and Beatrice Lacey that began in the 1960s is resurfacing today in the field of neurocardiology, the study of the heart brain. J. A. Armour asserted in his groundbreaking book, *Neurocardiology*:

> These scientific advances illuminate the fact that while we may believe the brain is our decision maker and ruler, the heart is more powerful than we ever imagined—functioning as a sensory organ, hormone-producing gland, and information-processing center.[21]

In *The Heart Speaks*, Mimi Guarneri, medical director of the Scripps Center for Integrative Medicine, gives us further evidence of the function of the heart:

> Each beat of the heart sends complex signals to the brain and other organs. These heart signals are capable of reaching higher brain centers, ultimately affecting our reasons and choices, our emotions and perceptions. Apparently, the heart has not only its own language but its own mind.[22]

Turning to God's Word for clarification on the function of the heart in decision-making, we find in Luke 6:45, "A good man brings good things out of the good stored up in his heart, and an evil man brings evil things out of the evil stored up in his heart. For the mouth speaks what the heart is full of."

Therefore, one of your main concerns as a parent should be to break through your child's innate proclivity to greediness found in their hearts to help them find the joy of giving and to experience the deeper satisfaction of making someone else happy rather than being concerned about their own happiness.

Will you choose greediness or gratefulness for your children?

Arrogance or Humility

We were told if we built our child's self-esteem, they would make wise choices. But the converse is true. Our child only becomes self-inflated to the point of arrogance, which leads to difficulty with friendships and relationships and cultivates a disrespectful attitude. A self-esteem-filled child can become aggressive, unkind, and disrespectful to family members, friends, and others in their lives.

Oh, but sweet humility is grown and cultivated from an emphasis on self-respect—that strong soul who isn't concerned with being first, who finds great joy in serving and helping others find their purpose, and delights in watching others learn what they've already learned. They are confident in knowing who they are, who they belong to, and what they stand for.

Which will you choose for your children . . . arrogance or humility? Insecurity or confidence? Self-exaltation or self-forgetfulness?

Fearful or Brave

My youngest granddaughters, at five and six years old, seem to have been born with mermaid tails. They would rather be in the pool than anywhere else. They have no fear of the water. It's a safe place for them. Years before, my son and daughter-in-law had enrolled each of the girls in an infant swim class in case of an accidental fall into the water. Consequently, they love the water.

It has been fun to watch the girls help other children overcome their fear of jumping off the diving board by showing them how to do it. Then waiting for their friend to take the jump. They are great encouragers, with shouts of, "You can do it! Come on, give it a try."

One act of bravery yields another and another. A spirit of fear is replaced with a desire to try new things in many areas of life because a child discovers that being willing to try is all you need to do it.

Which will you choose for your children . . . fearfulness or bravery?

Imitation or Authenticity

Mom and Dad, you can teach your children what you know, but they will learn more from what you model. To truly instill self-respect in your children, you must be a champion of respect. You must strive to be the person you want your children to become. If you want your children to be self-giving, they need to see your acts of benevolence toward others.

If you want your children to be resilient, you must get back up when you're knocked down to show your children how it's done. If you want your children to be content, you must be content. You can never expect more of your children than you do of yourself.

If you have cultivated self-respect within your own heart, you can lead your children with authenticity, which will lead them down the right path.

Which will you choose for your children . . . to be an imitation or the real thing?

Making It Real

Before I begin a parenting seminar, I often hear the following comment from a frustrated parent: "I'm doing what I was told to do, but it's just not working."

I usually nod in agreement. "I know, believe me, I know. You've been doing the best you could do under the circumstances. It's not your fault. You were given bad advice."

It is true. We've been following popular parenting advice for the last sixty years. Rather than raising a generation of well-adjusted, mature adults, we've raised a generation of adults who want someone to take care of them; while they play in the pigpen, we shake our heads in bewilderment.

This makes me think of a mom screaming at her rebellious teenage daughter in total disgust, "After all I've done for you, this is the thanks I get?"

If the disturbed teen could articulate what her heart is feeling, she would respond, "Mom, don't you see? This quest for my self-esteem has ruined me. I don't know how to take care of myself. I don't know how to get along. I don't know anything about life, Mom."

We entertained them without training them. The result has been devastating, evidenced by our fractured culture. Gerald Vann offers a good explanation, "When self-esteem is high, self-knowledge is very small."[23] My hope and prayer is that you will choose self-respect for your children and family.

In the chapters that follow, I will do my best to help you succeed in raising your children and teaching the children in your life to become StrongHearts, morally fit kids, grounded in truth and fortified with self-respect, who have not only head knowledge to lead, but heart knowledge to lead in the right direction, as they become all God created them to be.

CHAPTER TWO

Establish the Home of Respect

STRONG, adj. *The sense of the radical word is to stretch, strain, draw.*[1]

The greatest influence in a child's life is, has been, and always will be, the parents. That will never change. Our personal beliefs and our worldview, lived out in our behavior, affect the ease or difficulty with which our children experience finding their place in the world. Daily interactions. Attitudes felt and observed. Words spoken. Words left unspoken. Mannerisms emulated. Habits formed. Decisions made. Actions witnessed.

Before we can establish a home of respect, we must look in our own hearts and define the beliefs that shape our behavior, which becomes our worldview.

What Is "Worldview"?

Worldview comes from the German word *Weltanshauung*. *Welt* means "world," and *Anschauung* means "point of view," "opinion," or "perception."[2] In other words, a "vision of the world."

The National Institutes of Health defines worldview as "a collection of attitudes, values, stories, and experiences about the world around us, which inform our every thought and action."[3]

One social researcher offers further explanation: "A worldview is something that everybody has. Most people don't even realize it, but essentially, it's the decision-making filter that we use. It's the intellectual, emotional, and spiritual filter that helps us to understand and interpret and respond to every reality that we experience."[4]

An engaging way of explaining worldview that can be used with children of all ages can be found in Manners of the Heart's *Leaders by Example* high school program. We take students to an event space for a day of training and open with an interactive activity using sunglasses with different colored lenses.

The students are seated at large banquet tables with several pairs of colored glasses in the center of each table. The students are asked to put on a pair of glasses and look around the room. We then count down from ten to zero and ask them to pass the glasses to the right. It is amazing to watch students look around in bewilderment as the world around them seems to change with each different colored lens, when in reality it is only the lens that has changed.

After three or four rounds of switching glasses, I offer this thought: "We're here today to help you find a fresh viewpoint of the world around you, because the truth is, the world is good, bad, *and* ugly. Finding your place in the world will be determined more by how you choose to view the world than the state of the world."

The day continues with exercises that open the eyes of the students' hearts to see beyond themselves and their circumstances to the possibilities of who they can become. Ultimately, our goal is to help them develop a desire to find their purpose in life and the drive to pursue it.

Let's explore how you view the world and how your point of view was developed in your younger years, so you can help your children develop a worldview that will serve them well.

Who Are We?

Think back to your childhood . . . What comes to mind first? Good memories or bad? Do you cringe or do you smile when you look back to your beginning? What beliefs have lasted into adulthood that were planted in your heart by your parents?

How did you answer these fundamental questions of life: Who am I? Why am I here? Where do I come from? Where am I going? What is real? What is right and wrong? All of these questions were answered by the worldview you developed as a child that shaped your outlook and basic assumptions on life.

We've all had the experience of opening our mouths and hearing our parents' words come out, and usually, they're the very words we swore we would never say. It is important to understand how your childhood interactions shaped your approach to life and to parenting.

In other words, the viewpoint from which you interact with the world comes from your beliefs. Your beliefs shape your thoughts and behavior. That leads us right back to the reason for working in the heart of your child. The content of the heart formulates what you believe, what you think, say, and do.

For the sake of space here, I encourage you to visit jillgarnercontent.org/parents for a downloadable guide that will help you examine, in depth, the lessons you learned in childhood that inform your parenting decisions today.

Who Our Children Become

In tracking beliefs and behavior of children into adulthood, studies of social scientists have revealed that very little, if any, of a child's worldview changes.

In its nearly forty-year history, the Barna Group has conducted more than two million interviews over the course of thousands of studies on American culture. According to Barna Group's research:

- By the age of two, a child has already started developing their worldview.
- By the age of nine, a child's moral foundation is established.
- By the age of thirteen, a child's worldview is set in stone.[5]

The work of framing a child's worldview must be done in the youngest years. The older a child becomes, the more difficult it is to reframe an established point of view, especially if it is pointed in the wrong direction. Barna's research solidifies that of others—what a child believes about truth, forgiveness, and respect establishes their moral foundation. By the end of sixth grade, their worldview is nearly set and carries them into the tween years where those beliefs are refined and applied. As a tween moves into the teen years, beliefs become behaviors that are defended.

The older a child becomes, the more difficult it is to reframe an established point of view, especially if it is pointed in the wrong direction.

I taught sixth grade for many years and witnessed the transformation that took place in the hearts of my students during this pivotal year. When the year opened, I had a room full of rising sixth graders who hesitated to answer opinion questions for fear of judgment by their peers or me. By the end of the year, hands were raised to offer opinions before questions were even asked. Their timidity had been replaced by a willingness to test their opinions in light of what their peers believe.

I had the opportunity to spend time with many of my students in their high school years. The fear of what others might think about their opinions had been replaced with an eagerness to defend their point of view. For students headed in the right direction, it was exhilarating to witness the outpouring of a solid worldview. It was clear the beliefs instilled by their parents would lead them into a fulfilling adulthood.

It was equally sad to hear a perspective on life based in a damaging belief system that was sure to lead a confused teenager into deeper trouble as they entered adulthood.

Let me pause here and say—please don't feel discouraged if you're dealing with a teen who has veered off course. It *is* possible to redirect a confused teenager. It's the not knowing what went wrong that keeps you from finding the right answers for a wayward teen.

As we dig into the stages of a child's development in the rest of this chapter, you will be able to recognize where you could have lost your way, and hopefully, find answers to get you and your teen back on track.

The Home of Respect

In my first parenting book, *Raising Respectful Children in a Disrespectful World*,[6] I introduced the "School of Respect" using four distinct stages of child development:

1. Tots (birth to age two)
2. Tykes (ages three to five)
3. Tweens (ages six to twelve)
4. Teens (ages thirteen to nineteen)

Each stage has a different developmental goal with specific training methods. During each stage, children have two critical soul questions that need to be settled to prepare them for the next level of maturity. The soul questions get to the heart of the matter. If your child is struggling, chances are there is a soul question that has not been answered.

See the chart below for the lesson plan of the "School of Respect":

THE SCHOOL OF RESPECT		
Stage	Goal	Training
Tots: *Birth to two* Can I trust you? Who's in charge?	Trust	Establish routines Set a schedule Be the parent
Tykes: *Three to five* Are you watching me? Who do I belong to?	Security	Offer recognition Pay attention Show ownership
Tweens: *Six to twelve* Do you really love me? Are you real?	Obedience	Build relationship Offer effective discipline Be authentic
Teens: *Thirteen to nineteen* Who am I? Can I be in charge?	Self-Respect	Give responsibility Enable self-discovery Transfer accountability

We can't expect a two-year-old to trust what we say unless she is sure we are in charge. We can't expect a five-year-old to step into kindergarten with enough confidence to cross the threshold of the classroom unless he knows who he belongs to and that his parents are watching him.

Obedience in a twelve-year-old comes from a strong parental relationship grounded in love and fortified with admiration for a parent who is the same 24/7. Watching an eighteen-year-old graduate from high school confident of his next step in life is accomplished when he knows he is ready to be in charge.

Before we can put these lessons in place, we must go deeper to establish a foundation from which to build our home of respect. Let's consider for a moment what it takes to lay a foundation for a structurally sound home.

The Foundation for the Home of Respect

Strict building code standards must be met before a home can be occupied. A few of these elements are:

- Site grading
- Load bearing value of the soil
- Width of footing
- Levelness
- Strength of concrete

The most critical of these components is the strength of the concrete, which must have a minimum of 2,500 pounds per square inch of density to meet the building codes. Without this density, the weight of the home—including the structural elements, furniture, fixtures, possessions, and people—will cause the foundation to crumble under the load. Even a slight miscalculation or misconstruction can cause a house to be unstable.

In addition to the correct density of the concrete, rebar (short for a reinforced bar) is a steel rod used to bring greater stability to the concrete. The strength it provides to the load-bearing parts of the home makes it a necessity in building construction. Rebar helps maintain the structural integrity of the home and prolong its lifespan.

The primary purpose of rebar is to increase the tensile strength of the concrete slab, which helps to avoid cracking. Rebar is installed on the site as the foundation is being built. Concrete is then poured over it. With rebar imbedded in the concrete, the foundation is better able to resist breaking under tension.

The same is true for our families.

Respect, like rebar, enables a family to resist breaking under the wear and tear of everyday tensions. Mutual respect helps maintain and protect each family member's integrity. A respectful family environment builds trust and safety and creates a place of great joy.

Take another look at the "Home of Respect" chart with the undergirding of respect that takes place in each stage of development to support your family. In bold, you'll see the targeted goal for your child as they mature. The four sections that follow the chart discuss the development of respect in detail within each stage.

THE HOME OF RESPECT		
Stage	Goal	Training
Tots: *Birth to two* Can I trust you? Who's in charge?	Trust **Respect for parents**	Establish routines Set a schedule Be the parent
Tykes: *Three to five* Are you watching me? Who do I belong to?	Security **Respect for God**	Offer recognition Pay attention Show ownership
Tweens: *Six to twelve* Do you really love me? Are you real?	Obedience **Respect for others**	Build relationship Offer effective discipline Be authentic
Teens: *Thirteen to nineteen* Who am I? Can I be in charge?	Self-Respect **Respect for self**	Give responsibility Enable self-discovery Transfer accountability

In the Tot Years

Your infant is looking into your eyes wondering if you can be trusted. When you are consistently attentive to the basic needs of your child by setting a schedule, for instance, you are building trust. When your child doesn't have to scream to let you know he's hungry or fret uncontrollably because he's tired, you are building trust.

When you remove your two-year-old to a place of isolation until the wailing subsides from a temper tantrum, your child gains respect for your authority. When you stand in your place of God-given authority as a parent, your child can relax and just be a kid without having to worry about who's in charge. The first and most important understanding of respect is that respect cannot be demanded, it must be commanded by the choices you make.

Knowing that strong families are the building blocks of society, a community cannot be stable when its families are torn apart. Perhaps this is why the first of the Old Testament commandments concerning our relationship with others is "Honor your father and your mother." The more respect garnered for parents, the greater the degree of respect that will carry beyond the immediate family and into strengthening the community. Tim Keller said, "It's respect for your parents that is the basis for every other kind of respect and every other kind of authority."[7]

Here are three ways respect for parents can be instilled in children in the tot stage:

1. Be the parent who accepts your responsibility to train your child out of great love for your child.
2. Always look at your child when they speak to you. Get down on their level and look them in the eye. This is teaching respect by showing respect.

3. Train yourself to be calm when tensions mount with a strong-willed two-year-old. Be firm, but fair. Show respect to your child through kindness. Being firm about what needs to be done shows respect for your child and the value of the task at hand. If your two-year-old has a temper tantrum in public, kindly but firmly remove them from the situation.

   During a trip to the grocery store when my children were young, one of my sons lost it when I said no to his request for a chocolate cake in the bakery section. With as little emotion as possible on my part, we headed straight for the car, but rather than going home, I waited until he calmed down, and then went back into the store. I wanted him to understand that his disrespectful attitude would not change our plans.

As your child gains respect for you and your place of loving authority in their life, you are setting the foundation from which to build respect for God in your child.

In the Tyke Years

Not to put any pressure on you, but you are your child's first glimpse of God. How a child perceives God—as a loving father or an uncaring rule maker, as a kindhearted shepherd or a hard-hearted king—depends greatly on your child's interactions with you during the formative years from three to five. As you continue to build on the foundation of respect you have established from birth, you can mold your child's respect for God by how you "show" your child God's great love.

Here are six ways to help your child cultivate love and respect for God:

1. When you tuck your child in bed at night, teach them how to pray. More than teaching a rote prayer, teach them how to talk to God about their day. Teach them how to share what they're

thinking and what they're feeling with God. My sons, and now grandchildren, practice a simple routine of saying "Goodnight, Lord" as they close their eyes, and "Good morning, Lord" when they open their eyes. This is one of the first "holy habits" you can instill in your child's heart.

2. A beautiful way to grow respect for God in your child's heart is by helping them see how much God loves us. Use everyday happenings to point your child to God's care over us. For instance, when you hear a siren, stop and pray with your children for protection for those in need of help. A few months ago, two of my granddaughters were in the car with me when we had to pull over for a firetruck on call. The barely five-year-old shouted from the backseat, "God, follow that firetruck! Somebody really needs Your help!"
3. Teach your child what the Bible has to say about everyday issues. For example, when your child is scared, you can share that "God is with you always."
4. Keep your promises. If you said you would take your child for a walk when you finished a task, then do it. Let your child know you are a person of your word, just as God is a person of His word. This commands their respect for God's promises.
5. Just as you expect your five-year-old to ask politely, you should make requests of your child using kind language. Please and thank you should always be part of your speech to your child, being mindful they will emulate your words and your actions. You can remind them that God doesn't demand that we love Him but asks that we love Him in response to His great love for us.
6. Set an expectation with your child of saying "Yes, sir" and "Yes, ma'am" when speaking with adults. For those who wince at

> teaching this courtesy, let me "unwince" you. Teaching "Yes, sir" and "Yes, ma'am" is more than a common courtesy, it is your best opportunity to instill respect for authority in your children. Beyond respect for your authority, you are leading them to say "Yes, Sir" when God calls them by name.

Instilling respect for God at this stage solidifies your child's world-view. You are enabling them to see the world through a set of attitudes, stories, and expectations that inform their every thought and action. This is the beginning of a rising StrongHeart.

In the Tween Years

Your tween is looking to you and asking if you really love them enough to say no when no is the right answer: *Do you really love me enough to make the hard call when the easier call, in the moment, is to give in? Are you going to put boundaries in place that protect me and teach me the boundaries I need to put in place for myself?*

Your fourth grader is searching for his identity. Your fifth grader is looking for the place that satisfies her need for belonging. Instilling respect for others enables your children to get along better with their peers, which makes finding their place much easier.

Let me offer a few suggestions for instilling respect for others during these years of self-discovery:

1. Set boundaries and be sure your tween understands the limits and the consequences for choosing not to abide within the boundaries. In the same way, be certain your tween understands your expectations of helping them become all they are meant to be. (We'll dig into this in chapter 5.) The hard part isn't setting the boundaries and the expectations but upholding them when your child pushes back.

2. The simple act of expecting your tween to greet adults with "How are you?" and a smile with a handshake teaches children how to respect others.
3. Your child is watching you. How's your attitude? Do you have a positive attitude, or do you complain about petty disruptions? Do you use a respectful tone when interacting with the clerk who is rude? Do you return disrespect with respect in your interactions? At this stage of your child's development more than any other, they will emulate what they see in you. If you have a disrespectful tween, check your attitude first. If you've allowed yourself to take on a less than admirable attitude, admit your fault to your child and suggest you work on it together.
4. Mom, this is the age to instill modesty in your daughter as a form of respect for others and herself. If your daughter is comfortable in tiny swimsuits and too-short shorts as a tween, she won't think a thing about it when she's a teenager. While not ultimately responsible for the way others view her, choosing to act and dress in a respectful, Christ-honoring way provides another opportunity to show respect to those around her.
5. Dad, this is the age to instill respect for women in your son's heart. The way you treat his mom tells your son everything he needs to know about how to treat girls he is around, including his mom and sisters.
6. Let's not leave out grandparents. Just as we learned that teaching children respect for parents is the beginning of all respect, that holds true for grandparents. Visit or talk often. Make them a part of your everyday lives. Keep your children connected to their grandparents. Honor them with your time and love, which is respect at its best.

7. Quote Scripture and help your first grader begin to memorize God's Word. We have a memory box that stays in the kitchen. Inside is a set of index cards for the books of the Bible. I write a verse at the top of two cards and give them to the two granddaughters. They copy the verse and memorize it by repeating it several times. During the next couple of days, I ask them to recite it, reminding them that they are burying God's Word like a hidden treasure in their hearts for the day when they need God's truth to help them. When they have memorized the verse, we put it in the box and lock it to symbolize hiding God's Word in our hearts.

By the end of this stage, your child should have a clear understanding of respect for parents, God, and others. According to the Barna Group:

> A person's lifelong behaviors and views are generally developed when they are young—particularly before they reach the teenage years. While those foundations are refined and the application of those foundations may shift to some extent as the individual ages, their fundamental perspectives on truth, integrity, meaning, justice, morality, and ethics are formed quite early in life. After their first decade, most people simply refine their views as they age without a wholesale change in those leanings.[8]

Moving into the teen years, you'll see that sixth grade becomes the year of testing all you've poured into them thus far.

In the Teen Years

As we observed, at the beginning of this stage, children begin deciding for themselves what they will accept and what they will reject from their childhood. If they see that your beliefs are real and work for you, chances are great they will adopt those beliefs in their own lives.

In a 2020 Pew Research Center study of parents and teens from many religious and nonreligious backgrounds, 55 to 86 percent of teens reported they hold the same belief as their parents. Eighty percent of evangelical Protestants and 86 percent of religiously unaffiliated topped the list.[9]

If, in their questioning, they find gaps in us, they will search for something with no gaps. While we know the truth is that we can all be hypocrites, our teens must reconcile that fact within their own hearts. They haven't yet discovered that we are all flawed human beings.

My sons always had more questions than I had answers for, but the questioning reached a new height at this stage, just as it should. They were searching for their identity, not as my sons, but as their own persons. This is the reason middle school was such a tough season of life for most of us. Honestly, how many of us, if asked, would raise our hand to share a wonderful middle school story? It's a tough time of life.

Groups of friends become cliques that don't welcome outsiders. Lines are drawn in the sand. Cool kids in the circle, not-so-cool kids outside the circle. Athletes enter a world of their own. Smart kids are often ostracized. The kids who were already headed for trouble now have the freedom to get into *real* trouble.

While these groups are being formed, each child is searching for their individual identity. They're looking for the right fit that feels comfortable, not forced, like a piece of a complicated puzzle. They're looking for their place of belonging . . . for who they are, whose they are, and who they are meant to be.

Underneath it all, our hope as parents is that we are helping them develop self-respect that protects their hearts from the outside influences seeking to pull them in the wrong direction.

We should never think our teenagers can handle life on their own, even when they try to convince us they can. Yes, we must give them more responsibility with each year that passes, but they still need our guidance and direction as they navigate the turbulent waters of our confused culture.

They will welcome your guidance if, from birth, you satisfied the answers to their soul questions.* If not, do not fret. As I mentioned earlier in this chapter, it's never too late to help a wayward teen make the turn back. Knowing the soul questions that were missed will bring the first step toward healing.

Here are a few thoughts on helping your teen develop respect for self that insulates their heart and fortifies their soul without isolating them from the world they so desperately want to fit into.

1. Studies have shown that disrespect in teens is often rooted in too much screen time and not enough family time.[10] While I believe screen time should be minimal on a daily basis, everyone should unplug at least once a week to be a family. Everyone—Mom and Dad, that means you too. Studies have shown resentment builds in the younger years when children grow up competing with their parents' cellphones for attention that often erupts in the teen years in disrespect and rebellion.
2. Don't allow yourself to get caught in the trap of disrespect. Return disrespect with the surprising reaction of respect. Often, this simple act can deescalate an ugly moment in a split second. Sarcasm often creates soul wounds. Young children don't understand sarcasm, while teenagers perceive it as disrespect in their parents.
3. Maintain a few nonnegotiable rules but allow your teen to take on more responsibility for maintaining homework and

* For an in-depth study of the soul questions, visit jillgarnercontent.org for a downloadable study guide from *Raising Respectful Children in a Disrespectful World.*

expectations of commitments. Give in areas where you can, but hold the line in areas of critical importance, such as disrespectful behavior, whether in word or deed.

4. If/when your teen messes up, let all natural consequences fall in place. Never shield your teen from consequences of their wrong behavior. If you do, I guarantee you will set up your teenager for trouble that will last into adulthood.

For a child who has grown up with respect as the rebar of their foundation, their view of the world will be rock solid. A firm foundation of respect for you, God, others, and themselves will enable your child to become a StrongHeart who can withstand the onslaught of the world.

CHAPTER THREE

Replace Happiness with Joy

STRONG, adj. *Well-fortified; able to sustain attacks; Not easily subdued or taken; as a strong fortress or town.*[1]

In the 1960s, when parents were asked their deepest desire for their child, the most common response was for their child to grow up to be a good citizen. Just a decade later, the responses began to shift to their children finding contentment. Since the late 1970s, in survey after survey, the overwhelming response to the question "What do you want most for your children?" has been "to be happy."[2]

So, after fifty-plus years of seeking our children's happiness, are children happy yet? According to research, they're not. In fact, today's children are more unhappy than children have been in the last fifty-plus years. The statistics of the well-being of our young people are devastating:

- Suicide is the second-leading cause of death in ten to twenty-four-year-olds.[3]
- Fifteen percent of youth (3.7 million) ages twelve to seventeen are affected by major depression.[4]
- Research shows that up to 25 percent of students struggle with clinical anxiety, which can significantly impact a student's ability to learn and perform to capacity.[5]

- Fifteen million (7 percent) of American adults have Social Anxiety Disorder (SAD). The first symptoms of SAD appear during childhood or early teenage years for more than 75 percent of those affected.[6]
- One of the saddest statistics regrading today's children comes from the Centers for Disease Control and Prevention—one in five children, ages five to seventeen, more than fifteen million, have a diagnosable mental, emotional, or behavioral disorder in a given year.[7]

According to these statistics, chasing after happiness is a futile pursuit.

A hard truth is that parents whose deepest desire is for their child's happiness often raise the most miserable child. They believe keeping their child happy is their primary duty. But a parent's primary duty is *not* to keep their child happy, but to help their child discover joy—lasting joy that carries them through life's disappointments with hope.

Just as the *Merriam-Webster Dictionary* lists self-esteem and self-respect as synonyms, the same is true with happiness and joy. But, once again, I would like to propose that happiness and joy are also polar opposites. They cannot be used interchangeably, for the seeking after happiness and discovering of joy come from different pursuits with different outcomes.

I remember when my twin sons were born, I had a personal aversion to pacifiers. This may sound silly, but even the name "pacifier" bothered me. I didn't want to give my sons something to pacify them. I wanted to encourage their curiosity. I wanted my sons to engage with the world around them and I wanted them to learn contentment apart from being occupied. My mom friends thought I was crazy. One friend said I was setting myself up for misery because the boys' discontentment would be more than I could handle.

Instead, I found peace of mind in the decision because the boys found contentment in looking around at the world they had entered.

This is one way I found to help them learn to be content with their present set of circumstances. (Not to be overlooked, as infants, they were on a schedule, so they knew they would be fed before they were starving and enabled to rest before they were exhausted. Revisit the "Home of Respect" chart for the training method in the tots stage.)

A parent who focuses on happiness often becomes an obstacle to their child finding joy. If our greatest desire for our children is to be happy, we will do our best to help them avoid pain and disappointment with the giving of things to content them. Parenting expert John Rosemond wholeheartedly agrees that it isn't a parent's primary job to raise "a 'happy' child." He goes on to say:

> Your job is to raise a person who is respectful of others no matter their circumstances, compassionate, charitable, hard-working, trustworthy, and always puts forth his/her best effort. The road to self-sufficiency is paved with frustration, disappointment, failure, falling flat on one's face, and other equally "unhappy" experiences. We cannot afford to deny children these things.[8]

Rosemond makes it clear—unless our children are unhappy at times, they will not learn life lessons needed to mature. When we "fix" the problem for our children, we deny them the opportunity to "fix" it for themselves and learn while doing it. When we make our children's happiness our primary goal in parenting, we cannot help our children develop two legs to stand on, so they will look for crutches to lean on. The world is waiting with a variety of crutches, none of which we would ever want our children to choose.

Obsessed with the Pursuit of Happiness

How did we become obsessed with our children's happiness? We began esteeming our children rather than respecting them. We buried our children in stuff, numbed them with entertainment, and smothered them with attention, telling them they could be anything they wanted to be, do anything they wanted to do, and have anything they wanted to have. With all the best intentions, we began losing sight of our children's heart needs.

In the early 1900s, parents began buying teddy bears for their infants.[9] This new and sweet gesture to celebrate a newborn launched an explosion in the creation of toys for tots.

Even with the rise in toy choices in the 1920s, children still spent their days roller skating, acting out bad guys vs. good guys with their friends, playing with dolls, and riding bicycles. Reading was a favorite pastime. Boredom was not yet an experience understood by children. Organized sports for elementary children consisted of a pick-up game in a nearby vacant lot in the city or an open field in the country.

Then along came Disney, founded in the late 1920s for the purpose of bringing happiness to children's lives through animation. I admire how Walt Disney believed "the important thing is to teach a child that good can always triumph over evil."[10]

When Disneyland–California opened in 1955 as "the happiest place in the whole world," the entertainment of children took on a new meaning. McDonald's soon followed suit after the opening of Disney World–Florida in 1977 by introducing the world's first Happy Meal, a child-focused, highly caloric burger combination meal with toys and small giveaways.[11]

In the Baby Boomer generation of parents, an obsession with our children's happiness was evident. We crowned our children king or queen of the home and bowed in subservience to their every whim and then expected our children to be kind, giving, and well-behaved. But instead, many parents watched their children become unkind, selfish, and out-of-control without a clue as to how it happened.

Today, the generation raised to be adored and worshiped is raising their own children. But rather than possessing an obsession with their *child's* happiness, for many in this generation, their deepest desire is to continue *their own* reign as monarchs. No sacrificing their agenda for the sake of their children. Rather than creating a peaceful home as a respite from the world, too many in this generation of parents drag their children into their world of loud music, incessant partying, and fun, fun, fun. FOMO is being transferred to their children, which could be one reason that children are experiencing difficulties at even younger ages. The Centers for Disease Control and Prevention reports that "1 in 6 U.S. children aged 2–8 years (17.4%) had a diagnosed mental, behavioral, or developmental disorder."[12]

For these parents, their expectation of a child who is calm and obedient with a sweet attitude is nearly impossible for a child who is overstimulated, set up for defiance, and unable to focus because of the programming that has taken place in their hearts and minds in such a home environment.

Not to despair. It's not too late to turn it all around.

Let's examine how our obsession with happiness has taken over and what we can do to replace the obsession of happiness with a quest for joy.

Treats Are No Longer Treats

The *Oxford Dictionary* defines treat as "an event or item that is out of the ordinary and gives *great pleasure*."[13] *Merriam-Webster* tells us a treat is "an especially unexpected source of *joy*, a delight or amusement."[14]

What should be a treat has become an expectation. Let me illustrate:

> Scenario 1: Mom picks up the kids from school every afternoon. Occasionally, they head for a drive-thru for frozen yogurt or ice

> cream. No special reason. Just because. Mom is thanked for the unexpected delight!
>
> Scenario 2: Mom picks up the kids from school every afternoon. They get in the car, asking for frozen yogurt. Today, Mom has a box drink and homemade cookies. Even the homemade cookies are not enough to elicit a thank you, only complaints about not getting their "treat."
>
> Scenario 1: Grandma rings the doorbell. Excited grandkids run to greet her. They push and shove for a hug and a kiss, as they pull her to the sofa to share their latest adventure story.
>
> Scenario 2: Grandma rings the doorbell. Excited grandkids run to grab her purse. They push and shove each other to find the candy she always brings. No hug. No kiss. They grab the candy and run off to start a new adventure on their own.

When is a treat no longer a treat? When your child has an expectation that something should come their way, the line has been crossed.

My granddaughters caught me by surprise on a recent stop at the grocery. As soon as we crossed the threshold, they began asking for everything in sight.

"I want that book and that other one too."

"Look, GG, I want that stuffed kitty."

"Can we buy some pretty flowers?"

"Stop, GG, I have to have that ______________!"

The incessant requests quickly turned to begging, which escalated into tears as I continued to respond, "Not today, girls."

One of my precious girls even said with tears in her eyes, "But GG, we just want a treat!"

Believe it or not, I didn't give in, which for grandmas is nearly impossible. When the girls were finally buckled back in their car seats, I turned to have a chat. Fortunately, I had recently taught the girls the StrongHeart lesson. Our conversation went something like this:

"Girls, let's talk about what just happened in the store," I began.

"But, GG, I don't like going to a store, if I can't get what I want," said the oldest.

"Do you remember the picture of StrongHeart's heart?" I asked.

"I remember," the little one said, nodding.

Her big sister chimed in, "Me too."

"He broke his own heart by making wrong choices, right? Getting what you want all the time empties your heart because 'things' can't fill up your heart. The more 'stuff' you get, the more stuff you want." I finished by adding, "When you're thankful for what you get and appreciate when a treat comes your way, your heart doesn't need more. You can enjoy doing what you're doing with the person you're doing it with!"

Both girls nodded.

The next day, we had to make a quick stop on the way home from school. You can imagine I was a bit apprehensive as we stepped into the store. My heart filled with joy when neither of the girls asked for a thing. On the way home, my oldest granddaughter said, "GG, my heart feels good."

Recall the definition of a treat: "an unexpected source of joy." We become obstacles to our children experiencing joy when we make getting a treat an everyday habit or part of every outing.

Just decide to say, "Not today." No matter the pounding you receive, stick with it, without raising your voice, every time you have the opportunity, until the requests stop. (And they will, if you don't give in, not even once!) After you've had a few outings without a request, surprise your child with a real treat, just because! Joy will fill your child's heart because your child will feel the depth of your love.

Happiness vs. Joy

The stark contrast between happiness and joy can be seen in the chart below:

Happiness	**Joy**
Fleeting	Lasting
External	Internal
Empty	Full
Things	Relationship
Pleasure	Contentment

Prioritizing the pursuit of happiness doesn't lead your children to joy. Making your child's happiness your major goal as a parent could even prevent your children from experiencing joy. I recognize these are bold statements. Hang with me as I unpack the significance of this understanding for you. Exploring the examples of the contrasts listed in the chart will help clarify the need to shift from the pursuit of happiness to the quest for joy.

Fleeting, not lasting

Think about how quickly happiness becomes sadness. Your son is happy with his tower of building blocks until his sister builds a taller tower. Your daughter is happy with her hairstyle until a friend comes over with the latest new hair ornament. Happy one minute, sad the next.

The pursuit of happiness becomes a moment-by-moment endeavor. The constant monitoring of the happiness index is exhausting for parent and child.

External, not internal

If you're trying to always keep your child happy, you're not helping your child learn how to find intrinsic satisfaction. You're teaching them to look for extrinsic gratification—the need for something or someone to "make" them happy.

When they're the center of attention, all is good. When they've just been given the thing they begged for, all is good. But when they're not the center of attention, they're not happy because their happiness is dependent on the accolades of others. When they must hear no to a request, their happiness meter slides below the tolerance level, and they let you know it.

Empty, not full

It shouldn't surprise us that mental illness, depression, and anxiety rates are at an all-time high in our society. The desire to ensure the happiness of our children doesn't prepare our children for the trials and inevitable disappointments that life brings.

Our children are not wired to be worshiped. They are wired to worship God and find joy in the contributions they make in the lives of others. With every whim that is satisfied, they are robbed of the opportunity of finding joy in serving. The cycle of getting more, only to want more, empties your child's soul.

Things, not relationship

How many times have you witnessed the child who didn't get their way throw a tantrum in public? It's easy to fall into the trap of letting presents replace your presence. If our goal is to keep our children happy, we will give and give and give everything but our time, energy, and love. We'll spend our time on gift-giving rather than relationship-building.

When all is said and done, the trip to Disney World will be remembered, but the nights spent playing card games or sitting around the dinner table playing word games will shape who your child becomes. These are the memories that are treasured because these are the moments that touch your child's heart and nurture their soul.

Pleasure, not contentment

As we've already discussed, the more children are given, the more children want, which leads to chronic discontentment. The pleasure of the moment is overshadowed by the thought of what's next.

Rather than spend your time and money on the next greatest have-to-have toy, when your children make a request, suggest they add it to their birthday wish list. You'll teach them delayed gratification, which brings with it great wisdom.

When their birthday rolls around, you can pull out the list, and much to their surprise, the "must-have" things they had added to the list will have long been forgotten or have become unimportant. What an outstanding way to help them see the difference between a need and a want. As your children grow older, this training will become the foundation of teaching good money management.

My hope is that you've decided to leave the quest for happiness behind and that you're eager to explore the quest for joy. How do we redirect our efforts from focusing on happiness to cultivating joy? We stop entertaining and start training.

Train Rather Than Entertain

A parent's job is not to entertain their child but to train their child, to prepare their child for adulthood. To cultivate their imaginations from which all great endeavors grow. To instill heart attributes that promote the maturation process. To pour God's Word and truth into their hearts.

With little parental involvement, classic toys and board games, intermingled with independent outdoor play, filled the out-of-school hours in children's lives of the '50s and '60s. Dinner was held at the family table with lively conversation and, often, informal question-and-answer sessions that gave children the opportunity to learn life lessons. The family operated as a single unit.

The evolution of video games and the internet in the '80s began absorbing children's hearts and minds in mindless activities rather than meaningful interactions. The family began to lose its place of prominence in a child's life. Individual family members spent time alone in their rooms, connecting with "friends" in other places. Less and less time was devoted to those character-building conversations that are remembered into adulthood.

Moving into the '90s and fast-forwarding to today, you'll find the overscheduling of children, beginning at age three, adding to the lack of training. Family dinners are few and far between with sports practice, dance rehearsals, entertainment venues, and special events. Little time is left in a child's life for reflection, life lessons learned around the dinner table, or time spent memorizing passages of Scripture. Sitting with grandparents, listening to family stories of heroism and bravery are rare.

Too many of today's parents fill their children's time with activities that do not nurture their souls but only fill their minds temporarily while emptying their hearts incrementally. Without intentional time set apart to teach children moral values, children find their answers to life in the world of confusing ideologies and accept the lies of our culture as truth.

As the entertainment of children has increased and training decreased, mental health issues have risen at an alarming rate. Unless a child's heart needs are met, their mind cannot function in a productive way. Reasoning breaks down, anxiety rises, and problems can become overwhelming.

Striking a balance is critical to your child's well-being.

First, let's look at the glaring contrast between training and entertaining:

Entertaining	**Training**
Distraction	Focus
Immaturity	Maturity
Avoidance	Purpose
Fantasy	Truth
Dependent	Independent
Happiness	Joy

When you make a commitment to train rather than entertain your children, they will benefit from experiencing the difference between distraction and focus, avoidance and purpose, immaturity and maturity, dependent and independent play, technology use and imagination, and busyness and quiet time. This commitment will take a shift in your perspective. You'll find an explanation with helpful suggestions in the sections that follow.

Distraction or Focus

My husband and I learned this lesson during a weekend with our granddaughters. We observed firsthand how entertainment might cause a distraction rather than teaching our granddaughters to develop their focus.

The girls were spending the weekend with us while their parents were away. They were five and six at the time. My husband and I had entertainment planned all day Saturday, including the children's museum, followed by lunch and a visit to the zoo.

After breakfast, the girls asked to go in the backyard to swing. I followed them out to the swing set. The next thing I knew they were going in the house to retrieve the modeling clay because they needed to "make food for the new restaurant in town." In what had been the play fort only an hour earlier, the restaurant opened for business, with a full menu of spaghetti, pizza, and assorted desserts. After the girls served up a colorful meal, they decided to entertain us with original songs.

The rest of the day was filled with chalkboard art on the patio, a visit to the "jungle" behind the outdoor kitchen, and delivery of love notes to stuffed animals who had moved into newly constructed cardboard box houses "in the neighborhood" around the yard. The girls made deliveries on tricycles transformed into mail delivery trucks!

The grand lesson we learned that day from our granddaughters was that the pleasure we wanted to give them through entertainment was nothing compared to the joy they experienced through their imaginations! The entire day was spent in one creative activity after another. We never left the house except to go back and forth outside for more supplies.

At the close of the day, one of the girls said, "GG, this was the best day ever," as she drifted off to sleep—content as she could be.

Without the distraction of entertainment, the girls' imaginations were brought into sharp focus for the tasks at hand.

Avoidance or Purpose

Two of our grandsons had just arrived at our house when the seven-year-old turned and said, "GG, can we play a video game?" Before I could respond, his ten-year-old brother stepped in front of his brother's face, put his hands on his shoulders, and said, "We don't do that at Paw-Paw and GG's. Get over it."

The seven-year-old shrugged his shoulders, then turned and ran to the sports box on the back porch, grabbed a baseball glove and ball and said, "Let's throw."

I was proud of both boys. (Before the older brother stepped in, I was going to suggest he could build a castle in the playroom rather than play a video game!)

My hang-up with video games is that too often gaming is a way to avoid building real relationships, especially in boys when they're allowed to hang out in their room with the door closed, plugged into a machine, and not plugged into life.

As of 2022, there were 215.5 million active gamers in the US, which represents 66 percent of the US population. Seventy-one percent are under eighteen. Roughly 8.5 percent of kids eight to eighteen years old have signs of video game addiction.[15]

If your child is more interested in playing video games than participating in activities with others in their free time, find out why. Is it to . . .

- Just have fun?
- Meet people online rather than in-person?
- Avoid spending time with the family?
- Hide from difficult emotions, experiences, or people?

The best antidote to video games is to get your teen involved in a passion that connects them with people and helps them find their purpose. A few more ideas to train rather than entertain include encouraging your child to:

1. Join a club or sports team
2. Enroll in art, dance, or music lessons
3. Get a pet and take primary responsibility for its care
4. Read a good book at the library
5. Take a class at the local community center
6. Participate in a church youth group
7. Volunteer to serve food, maintain public hiking trails, clean up the beach, or some other project[16]

Immaturity or Maturity

A five-year-old's birthday was fast approaching. Her mom asked what kind of party she wanted for her "extravaganza." Much to the mom's surprise, her daughter replied, "I don't want a big party, Momma."

"But honey, don't you want a party like all your friends?" Momma replied.

"No. I don't like the noisy music," her daughter answered.

"We don't have to have loud music," Momma said.

"Why are there so many grown-ups at a kids' party anyway?" the astute daughter asked.

"They like to celebrate birthdays," Momma responded. "What would you like to do for your birthday?"

"I want a friend to come over. We can paint and play. That would be more special than a bunch of people making a lot of noise."

Whoa, the maturity of a five-year-old! I happen to know this five-year-old had just attended back-to-back parties that were totally out of control. She had been part of the craziness. She had witnessed the stack of gifts, too many to keep. She had felt the isolation of the birthday girl who didn't feel honored but lost in the chaos.

Mom and Dad heard the cry of their daughter's heart and chose to get off the entertainment train. The most beautiful part of the story is that others got off at the next stop too. The new birthday party in this circle of friends is an at-home sleepover with one or two friends rather than an extravaganza. It only took one set of parents willing to do the right thing for others to follow.

The now six-year-old thanked her parents profusely when her little friend went home the next morning. She hugged them and said, "This was better than a party!" Far beyond happiness, she also experienced joy in her heart.

Aren't most of us just waiting for someone else to buck the norm, so we don't have to be the first? You can be the one to lead others in the right direction, beginning with your own children.

Dependent or Independent Play

Middle school teachers tell me a large percentage of their students struggle with weak problem-solving skills and a lack of motivation. Both can be addressed in the younger years through independent play.

Independent play takes place without technology or adult intervention. Through unstructured time, children investigate the world around them. Think of the two-year-old who stoops to examine a caterpillar, then listens to a bird sing, and stoops again to watch a bug crawl on the ground. I remember going to the park with my twin sons at this age. It took twenty minutes to walk from the car to the entrance because of all the "look at that, Mom" moments.

Given the opportunity to interact with their environment, children gain problem-solving skills by figuring out how things work or how to overcome an obstacle. This might look like a six-year-old who tries and tries again until he finally figures out how to maneuver the monkey bars. Or a ten-year-old who builds a building block creation without the instructions.

Independent play is a critical component of helping your child experience joy—joy that comes from discovering what they can do on their own. How sad it is when children are not given this opportunity due to technology and overscheduling by parents.

Technology Use or Imagination

Children need one to two hours a day of unstructured play without technology, either alone or with siblings and friends. The more time children spend playing without technology, the less they want technology. The sense of accomplishment that comes from building something from your imagination versus winning an electronic game is immeasurable.

Technology entertains children, but it doesn't train them in life skills. Technology creates a dependency that is hard to break. At a conference recently, I watched a child, still in a stroller, who was mesmerized by a handheld game. I was shocked when his mom said he was only two years old. While she browsed the exhibit booths and chatted with other moms, he was perfectly content to stare at the device until it ran out of life. Immediately, he began kicking and screaming for more. He could not be consoled until his mom put another device in his hands.

This dependence on technology carries over into the teen years. Katie Ely of Parenting with Focus offers this advice for teenagers:

> For older kids, independent play looks a little different, but they still need to have it. It's a time with no screens for an hour or two a day. The American Academy of Pediatrics recommends that teens get at least an hour of physical activity a day. Make your teens go outside and go for a walk, or play basketball, or ride their bikes. For inside entertainment, they could play cards, or lift weights, or start a hobby. Or here's a good one: They could look for a job. But the point is, they need to learn how to occupy themselves productively without screens.[17]

In addition to allowing their children too much technology, including TV and movie watching, many parents have been fooled into believing they must enroll their child in extracurricular activities by the age of three.

Busyness or Quiet Time

The old adage of too much too soon is applicable to our children's calendars. Children who live from one event to the next are in danger of expecting someone or something to entertain them. They become like a junkie who needs another hit to satisfy their unquenchable appetite for excitement.

Without the ability to self-direct their time, children become easily bored. When children are unable to occupy themselves, trouble soon follows. Research has shown that as kids get older and are unable to entertain themselves, they look to other things to amuse themselves like drugs, alcohol, and sex.[18] This can be one reason children from "good" homes with lots of attention, scheduled extracurricular activities, and constant stimulation get into trouble in the teen years. They have been programmed to be dependent on entertainment. In a sense, they have become addicted to busyness and don't know how to occupy their time in contemplative pursuits.

Encouraging children of all ages to play independently with unstructured quiet time reaps many benefits:

- They learn constructive ways to overcome boredom.
- They develop problem-solving skills.
- They have time to decompress from all the busyness.
- They develop self-respect in discovering what they can do on their own.
- They gain confidence to try new things without fear of failure.

In *Kids Say the Darndest Things*, a classic television show of the 1950s, host Art Linkletter offered these words of wisdom in combating the entertain versus train dilemma:

> The really important rule in bringing up children is to train them lovingly, demand their obedience and don't frustrate them unnecessarily. What really matters is the relationship between the child and his parents. It is how we feel deep down in our hearts toward our children that really counts. A child will endure pain, disappointments, and even fear, if he is loved. And his intuitive perception cannot be fooled. Training by love is a quick way to say it.[19]

True Happiness Is Real Joy

With a relaxed, almost irreverent demeanor, actor Matthew McConaughey delivered a remarkable speech to a graduating class at the University of

Houston a few years ago. Unlike most college commencement speakers, he chose to take off the suit coat, roll up his sleeves, and perch on a wooden stool to reach the hearts of the apprehensive students.

Sharing thirteen points of wisdom he had learned in his journey of life, his take on the difference between happiness and joy was, no doubt, something many of these students had never heard before.

> Happiness is an emotional response to an outcome. If I win, I will be happy. If I don't, I won't. It's an if then, cause and effect, quid pro quo standard that we cannot sustain, because we immediately raise it every time we attain it. . . . And I say if happiness is what you're after, then you're going to be let down frequently and you're going to be unhappy much of your time. Joy, though, joy is a different thing. It's something else. Joy is not a choice. . . . Joy is the feeling that we have from doing what we are fashioned to do, no matter the outcome.[20]

If you're like me, you may have to read these words a few times very slowly and ruminate on the last two sentences for a bit. If you do, I bet you'll agree with Mr. McConaughy's assessment of happiness and joy, as I do.

Joy brings strength to carry your child through times of disappointment. If your child is discouraged, it won't take much to bring them down. The Bible teaches that "a cheerful heart is good medicine, but a crushed spirit dries up the bones" (Prov. 17:22).

It has been said that joy is emotional energy that produces strength. Have you ever had a coach give you an inspirational speech? Have you been given a pep talk before a big performance? We know before the game starts or the curtain goes up the person who is geared up for the task at hand has a much better chance of performing well than the one who is feeling down. Studies have shown the impact of joy in a person suffering from a physical ailment or living with chronic pain versus one who is discouraged.[21] Watching a child who was just hurt on the playground bounce right back when a friend suggests a new game confirms that even pain can be forgotten in the presence of joy.

True Happiness

As joy decreases, strength decreases. As joy increases, strength increases. The Christian parent knows the source of true happiness and strength is faith in Jesus Christ. Nehemiah 8:10 says, "The joy of the LORD is your strength." Focusing on instilling the joy of the Lord in your child's heart is the first step toward raising a StrongHeart. Joy, not happiness, is the insulation your child's heart needs for protection from the world's discouragements.

CHAPTER FOUR

Instill a Heart of Gratitude

STRONG, adj. Powerful; forcible; cogent;
Adapted to make a deep or effectual impression on the mind or imagination.[1]

South Louisiana has been my home for more than thirty years—the land of crawfish, swamps, alligators, the delightful American-French Creole dialect, and the best food on the planet. Nothing characterizes Louisiana more than Mardi Gras, which has always been a strange phenomenon to me, a native Mississippian.

With the intention of marking the beginning of the Lenten season, Mardi Gras quickly became an irreverent mishmash of celebration and sacrifice. A season of revelry and rebellion before weeks of giving up something precious to focus on the coming commemoration of Jesus Christ's death, burial, and resurrection. Talk about conflicting messages!

My point in bringing up Mardi Gras is to look at a tradition that surrounds "the greatest free show on earth." Elongated barges on wheels, decorated as extravagant floats, each carry dozens of people through the streets of New Orleans. The parade goers line the sidewalks and throw their hands in the air, hollering, "Throw me something, Mister. Throw me something" to the masked riders as the floats go by. Others shout, "Give me something, Mister. Give me something," hoping for a treat of beads, cups, balls, or trinkets. At times, when a special "throw" is tossed, parents fight to retrieve the "prized" treat for their child.

Author Gary Sernovitz, writing in the *Wall Street Journal*, describes his experience of riding on a Mardi Gras float:

> A few spectators are happy to admire the parade floats for their ever-changing themes. Others, including children, the chief constituency of Mardi Gras parades, are there to catch the "throws": plastic beads, glass beads, coin "doubloons," plastic cups, plush toys, balls, sunglasses, and any other trinket a krewe can think to stamp its name on. But riding on a float is one way adults can be as gleeful as children. Sometimes the rider chooses to throw to a quieter kid, sometimes the more raucous. Some recipients demand a particular throw. Others don't say a word. I remember dozens of connections made in an instant of eye contact: a tourist couple shyly surprised at the stuffed animal in their hands, a father appreciative that his anxious daughter had finally caught a throw. For the first and maybe last time in my life, I was Santa Claus—every five seconds. [2]

Most riders agree with Sernovitz, there's nothing as exhilarating as making the wish of a child come true in the moment.

In the days following the parades, there are as many beads and trinkets left behind in trees and ditches as in the bags taken home. Just as quickly discarded as received.

We have just moved out of the parade season as I'm writing today, so the images are fresh in my mind. I can't help but think about the fact that our children have the same relationship to us and the world as the children at the Mardi Gras parades. With open hands, they proclaim, "Give me something, Mister. Give me something." They look to us and the world to be Santa and his elves, lavishing them with trinkets that will soon become meaningless and worthless throwaways.

As the Mardi Gras parades illustrate, in today's world, a treat is no longer a treat, just a trinket.

A Trinket or a Treat

We touched on this subject in the previous chapter. Let's dig a little deeper. *Merriam-Webster* defines a trinket as "a thing of little value."[3] A trinket is easily tossed aside because it has no special place in the heart of the one holding it. Here today, gone tomorrow without emotional attachment. And yet, in that moment, your child's heart wanted it.

A treat is something altogether different. Again from *Merriam-Webster*, we find an understanding of the difference in the definition of treat, "an especially unexpected source of joy, delight, or amusement."[4] Do you see the difference? A trinket is expected, sought after, asked for, and received with a greedy heart. A treat is given without expectation, without anticipation, and received with gratitude.

You know you've crossed the line from treat to trinket when your children have an expectation of getting something when you go somewhere. Rather than being grateful for what comes their way, they are greedily expecting something to come to them. They're looking for it, even waiting for it. You can turn this around. It won't be pleasant at first, but it can be done.

When Treats Become Trinkets

I've never forgotten the day my sons began learning that a treat is no longer a treat when it is expected. It has stayed with them into adulthood.

I had fallen into the trap of buying a treat for the boys—a candy bar or a Hot Wheels car on trips to the store. I recognized it had gotten out of hand because the boys anticipated they would get something every time we ran errands. No longer was my treat a treat; it had become an expectation. A nasty attitude of entitlement was taking root in their hearts.

Rather than hearing "pick something out," as they had been accustomed to hearing; this time, I said, "not today" to their request for a treat.

Oh my, you would have thought I was terrorizing them in the middle of the store. But I endured their chorus of disgust all the way to the car because I had made the decision enough was enough. (In case you're wondering, I've not found an easy way to change directions with this issue. You must go cold turkey and stick to your resolve, regardless of the upset.)

I did it again and again, trip after trip to the store, until they finally stopped asking.

Then, one day as we neared the checkout, I said, "Let's get a treat today!" The looks on their little faces spoke ten thousand words. They looked at each other in total amazement, as if to ask, "Is this a trick?"

I smiled, and added, "Pick out two treats. One to give and one to keep," which really confused them!

I gave each son money to pay for their treats. As soon as each had completed his purchase, I asked them to find someone to whom they could give a treat. One son gave a Hot Wheels car to a younger boy who lit up with excitement. The other son gave his favorite candy bar to a young girl who gave him a hug of gratitude.

"Wow, Mom, that was awesome," exclaimed Boyce.

"Yeah, that was super cool," added Chad.

Can you guess what happened the next time we went to the store? The boys asked if we could do it again. I said, "No, not today. We'll do it again another day." They accepted my answer with disappointment, but without fussiness.

The next time they asked, it wasn't for themselves at all, but to give something away.

When children experience for themselves that it truly is better to give than to receive, the transformation of turning their hearts from greed to gratitude begins. With each incident of giving without expectation of return, children develop a desire to serve. It doesn't take long before they stop thinking of what they can get and focus on what they have to give.

Take the Bad Stuff Out of Your Heart First

Manners of the Heart kids learn in pre-K that you must "take the bad stuff out and put the good stuff in" to rid your heart of the stuff that keeps you from finding joy.[5] If pre-K kids can learn it, we can too. To begin, we need to take a look at the innate greediness that resides in our own hearts. Not for our sake, but for the sake of our children.

We teach our kids the importance of "things" by how much we value "things." Before you attempt to work in your children's hearts, do your own heart check first. Search your soul with honesty and resolve, and then answer these questions:

- Do you want more money for the purpose of buying more or giving more?
- Do you repair or replace appliances when "technical" problems happen?
- Do you give something to the kids in front of Walmart? The Salvation Army bell ringer?
- Do you have to have the latest model car?
- Are you faithful to tithe to your local church?
- Do you own your money or does your money own you?
- What are you most thankful for?[6]

If your answers revealed the need to tame the greedy monster in your own heart, consider the following suggestions for how to do so:

- Be satisfied with last year's whatever. Let your children see that you don't toss things aside because they're used. They need to see that as things become old, they become more precious, rather than obsolete. (Don't you want them to feel that way about you when you're old and gray?)

- Pay as you go. Rather than pull out your plastic, teach your children by example that it's better to pay as you go, which means saving for purchases, rather than buying on credit. Help your children weigh the pros and cons of purchases. Delayed gratification often changes "I have to have it" to "I'd like to have it" to "I don't need it."
- Resist the comparison trap.
- Make a list of what/who is most important in your life. Count your blessings, name them one by one.
- Follow my sweet husband's lead and thank the clerk at the store, thank the server in the restaurant, thank your neighbor for being a good neighbor. Thank God for a beautiful sunset . . . all in front of your children.
- Live with the glass half full perspective. When it rains and ruins an outing, let your kids know you're thankful for the rain because the plants needed heaven's water.
- Write thank-you notes yourself. Explain to your children to whom a thank-you note is being sent and why, and then let the children stamp the envelope.
- Consider what you want to leave behind. Is it good memories of time spent with loved ones? Is it a life well-lived for others? Is it accumulated stuff? I helped a relative sort through her home after her husband died. We took pictures and pictures of the "stuff" they had accumulated over forty years in the same house, much of which they were saving for children and grandchildren. Most of his possessions were of no interest to any of their six children. The things he treasured were just trinkets to others.

If I could encourage you in one area of growth it would be to accumulate relationships, not things. Not only will your life be much richer, but the lives of your children will be richer by the example you set for them. Look for how much of yourself you can give, rather than how much you can get.

Giving, Not Getting

One of the great timeless truths is that life is a paradox, as evidenced in these thoughts:

- "It is more blessed to give than to receive" (Acts 20:35).
- We find ourselves when we come to the end of ourselves.
- Meeting disrespect with respect gains respect.
- Fear and bravery are two sides of the same coin.
- The more deeply you fall in love with yourself, the more unlovable you become.
- The more you fail, the more opportunity you have to succeed.

As discussed in previous chapters, the truth is we gain what we give away. We gain respect by giving respect. We find joy by making others happy. The same is true of gratitude. When we give generously of ourselves, our hearts grow in gratitude. If you want to know the satisfaction of gratitude, you must give generously of yourself.

Giving Yourself Away

A special family who radiates a beautiful spirit of gratitude and generosity comes to mind. This past summer, all but one of the children, eight total, helped their mom host a Vacation Bible School for more than two hundred children in kindergarten through fifth grade.

They transformed the gym of their local church into the days of ancient Jerusalem with tents, artisans, musicians, and even a camel. The entire week ran like the Olympics. Everything was on time, the individual team members operated at their maximum capabilities, and children were inspired to work hard and serve others with the gifts they had been given.

Ranging in ages from seven to twenty-one, some of the boys were centurions; others were townsfolk. The girls were dancers and helpers. I never saw rolled eyes or bad attitudes from the teenagers. Only humility and generosity. I asked Roxanne, the mom of this family, "How do you instill generosity and gratitude in your children?" Roxanne shared:

> Practice gratefulness . . . a good work ethic establishes a foundation for gratefulness. Children need to learn what it takes to make things happen. I am a big proponent of chores. They get an allowance in their accounts, but they don't get money for doing their "duties." They can earn extra money by doing chores that are beyond their responsibility as a family member.
>
> At Christmas, we take turns opening gifts one at a time. After a gift is opened, the recipient goes to the giver to express his/her thanks in the moment. I've taught my children that even if you don't like the gift or you already have it, you are to express heartfelt thanks to the giver. I try to help them understand that they're not thanking the giver for the gift, they're thanking them for the great love behind the gift, the kindness and generosity in giving the gift. I try to keep them focused on the person's heart, not the present.
>
> We write thank-you notes between Christmas and New Year's. Even siblings receive a thank-you note, not just grandparents and extended family.
>
> But the bottom line is chores. Regarding the results of doing chores, we get a lot of compliments that our children are hard-working kids! They usually do what they are asked without complaint. They are willing to volunteer to help when they see a need. Some of our children

> notice needs more than others as their personality and giftedness are bent in that direction, but I know having them participate in household chores has developed a good work ethic and a serving attitude.
>
> Chores teach children valuable life skills and the joy of serving others. When children participate in the running of the family household, they have a greater sense of belonging and ownership. In a large family, chores are not an option; they are a necessity!
>
> As a mom, I know it's easier to just do it yourself rather than train kids to help clean and cook, but we need to see the greater value in chores. It's not just about keeping the house clean, it's more about training our children to serve others and do a good job. Doing chores is a really great way to build self-confidence in our children.[7]

Roxanne was quick to point out that raising good children has more to do with parent training than child training.

Parent Training

I recently listened to an outstanding presentation by Kelly Butler, CEO of the Barksdale Institute for Reading, that left me nodding in agreement. She shared the great success Mississippi has found in moving from fiftieth to twenty-first place in fourth grade literacy in the last five years due to a broad effort that includes increased teacher training and old-fashioned phonics instruction.

One of the most impactful statements Butler made was this: "We have removed the excuses. We *do know* how to teach reading. Ninety-five percent of children can learn to read, if taught well. We need to implement the solution everywhere. All children can learn to read. They just need the right instruction that every child deserves."[8]

I couldn't help but think the same is true when it comes to parenting. Parent training is paramount to child training, isn't it? Children can learn if parents give the right instruction. Just as Mississippi reading proponents discovered, it wasn't that children were lacking in their ability to *learn*, they were lacking in the kind of instruction they needed to *learn to read*.

My hope is that as we continue to work through ways to raise a StrongHeart that you, too, will discover it's not so much about training your child as it is about training yourself!

Giving Too Much and Expecting Too Little

We've already looked at the obsession with self-esteem as a hindrance in raising capable children. With the Baby Boomer's desire to make our children happy—one goal in our focus on self-esteem—we neglected some of the valuable lessons we'd been taught. For example, writing thank-you notes was eventually considered an unnecessary exercise. Not looking someone in the eye and saying thank you for small gestures was excused. Standing when an adult entered the room and speaking to them as a form of gratitude for their visit was dismissed as antiquated.

Another outcome of the self-esteem movement was that parents didn't expect their children to do chores in their quest to make life easy for them. But we now know that not doing chores has been found to be detrimental to the maturation process, causing stress, anxiety, and a sense of entitlement, as evidenced in today's workplace.[9] A poorly developed work ethic is the number one complaint of employers.[10]

Amazing, isn't it, that a seemingly small thing like doing chores can either help create or prevent problems as children become adults.

If you were fortunate to have parents who expected you to participate in helping your family, you may see the difference in your peers who were not expected to. Here are some examples:

Those who did not do chores	**Those who did chores**
Lazy	Responsible
Can't-do attitude	Can-do attitude
Makes excuses for not trying	Willing to try and fail
Can't figure things out	Problem-solver
Lacking in life skills	Proficient life skills
Lacking in contribution	Value and joy in contribution
No work ethic	Strong work ethic

Children don't need to be pampered; they need to be prepared for life. This lack of preparation can instill resentment toward the person who is giving a child everything but expecting too little in return.

Chores Keep Life in Balance

Another aspect of the importance of chores is that chores help keep the most important things in life the most important. As Baby Boomers began replacing significance in life with success in life, we pushed our children to get into the best colleges to have the best opportunities for "success." In doing so, we neglected the education of their hearts.

We told our children their only job was to study. We did everything for them, including things they should have done for themselves. We turned all their attention inward. Rather than helping them see that relationships are more important than achievement, we sent the opposite message. We also said, without saying it, doing whatever it takes is acceptable. (We'll talk more about this when we discuss integrity.)

Until the 1990s, the validity of chores for children was understood. Children were expected to perform chores because they were a contributing member of their family. As parents began placing more importance on academic and athletic achievement, they allowed chores to take a lesser place to homework and sports practice.

By 2015, a survey of parents showed 82 percent reported they did chores as a child, but only 28 percent expected their children to pitch in and help. In addition to sports and academics, some of the reasons for not assigning chores included not wanting to hear children complain; being a perfectionist who couldn't handle anything less than perfection in folding clothes and making beds; or being too busy to teach their children how to manage their chores.

Commenting on the study, psychologist Richard Rende wrote, "Parents want their kids spending time on things that can bring them success, but ironically, we've stopped doing one thing that's actually been a proven predictor of success—and that's household chores."[11]

In 2019, Rebecca Sharf and Mark DeBoer, developmental pediatricians at the University of Virginia, published the Early Childhood Longitudinal Study, in which 9,971 children participated. Within the study, parents of kindergartners reported the frequency with which their child performed chores. In the third grade, these children responded to a questionnaire regarding their perceived interest or competence in academics, peer relationships, prosocial behavior, and life satisfaction. The children also completed direct academic assessments in reading, math, and science.

DeBoer concluded, "Families that see the importance of chores are more likely to have children who do better in school, feel better about chores, and feel better about themselves. The children that never had chores were the lowest in everything—lowest peer relationships, and lowest life satisfaction. So definitely . . . all kids should have some chores."[12]

The Harvard Grant Study, begun in 1938 and continuing today, has followed 724 young people who became high achievers. Of the many interesting findings that have come from the extensive research is that the most successful participants in the study did chores as children. It wasn't affluence or education that determined their success in building healthy relationships and a strong work ethic, but the lessons learned from participating in their family of origin through doing chores.

Chores for the Family Create Gratitude

Our resident chore expert, Roxanne, pointed out that chores give children the opportunity to experience the joy that comes from serving. As children serve each other in the home, they develop an understanding of cooperation and collaboration—the give and take of serving and being served from which gratitude bubbles. Gratitude is an internal characteristic and generosity is our external expression of our sense of gratitude. Gratitude is how we feel, and generosity is how we express that feeling to the world.

Through this process, children develop a deep sense of belonging, satisfying two of their soul questions, which leads to gratitude.

Instilling gratitude in the hearts of your children involves assigning chores because:

- Life skills are learned that carry them into adulthood
- They understand a sense of God's purpose and presence in their lives
- Relationship skills are developed that bring connection to others
- They learn patience in delayed gratification

In the process of doing age-appropriate chores, children:

- Gain competence and confidence in their own abilities
- Discover talents to be developed
- Feel valued for their contributions to the family
- Learn self-discipline by doing what they don't want to do with excellence

My seven-year-old granddaughter asked to wash the dishes after supper last week. I smiled and said, "Absolutely, thank you for your help." Her response, "It feels good to wash dishes for my family." Truth from the heart of a child. You'll see in the suggestions listed below, her heartfelt joy in helping was the natural outflow of chores.

Chores for Tots to Teens

I've compiled suggestions for age-appropriate chores to help get you started:

Tots (ages two to three)

Children love to imitate adults at this stage. This is the right age for child-sized cleaning sets and "adult-like" chores:

- Get clothes out for bedtime
- Pick up toys after playing, put books on shelves (not so their room is clean, but so that no one comes in and trips over anything)
- Put laundry in the washing machine

Tykes (ages three to five)

- Help with cookie baking, bread baking
- Set the table
- Make the bed
- Help with putting away groceries
- Sort laundry by color
- Dust lower shelves

Pretweens (ages six to ten)

- Make lunch for school
- Take out the trash

- Vacuum/sweep floors
- Help with the dishes
- Laundry
- Water plants
- Feed pets

Tweens (ages eleven to twelve)

- Do the laundry
- Vacuum/mop the floors
- Yardwork

Teens (ages thirteen to nineteen)

- Wash the car
- Mow the lawn
- Plan and prepare meals
- Pressure wash/clean windows
- Babysit
- Clean the bathroom

Open Hands and Open Hearts

"It's mine! Give it back," sister snaps when her brother tries to snatch a toy out of her hand.

"I want to play with it," brother shouts back.

"But I'm playing with it right now," sister counters.

Brother digs deeper, "You're mean."

"No, I'm not," sister retorts.

"Yes, you are," brother snorts.

Sound familiar?

The two-year-old tot phase of "Me and Mine" can be used to your advantage, and theirs, in helping to open your child's heart to giving with a grateful heart. Chuck Kalish, PhD, at the Study of Children's Thinking Lab at the University of Wisconsin, explains this phase and one way a parent might respond to a scenario such as a "tussle over toys":

> Clearly say to your child, "This truck is yours and that car isn't." No explanation. No discussion. Even in the toddler years, your child can keep track of what belongs to whom. As kids get a little older, they will discover that it feels good to make someone else happy by sharing their own toy with someone else.[13]

One of my favorite exercises to open a child's heart to the difference between giving and receiving is to propose the following scenario:

> "Last week someone made your all-time favorite cookies. I don't mean slice-and-bake or add-water-to-the-mix cookies. I mean, real homemade cookies." I continue, "A friend comes by to see you. There are only two cookies left on the plate . . . a nice, big cookie and a small cookie that must have been the last bit of dough. Your friend is eyeing those cookies. What will you do? Will you offer your friend the big cookie or the little cookie?"

Here are a few of the real responses I have heard from children:

- "I'd give 'em the little cookie, of course."
- "I don't have to give 'em a cookie. They both belong to me."
- "I'd give 'em the little cookie, so they know who's boss."
- "On a good day I might break them both in half and make things equal."
- "I know you want me to say that I'd give 'em the big cookie, but hey, I gotta take care of myself first."
- "I'd give away the big cookie, 'cause it would feel good."

Your children will experience firsthand the joy of living with an open heart toward others.

More Than Chores

Instilling gratitude in your children's hearts is a process. There will be victories and defeats, ups and downs, successes and failures. Just remember you and your children are in this together.

Amy Morin, LCSW, suggests making it a habit to regularly express gratitude in your family. Here are some examples from Morin of rituals you might establish:

- Everyone takes turns during dinner sharing one thing they're grateful for from their day.
- At bedtime, ask each child to say three things they feel grateful for.
- During the car ride to school, everyone thanks someone else in the car for something.
- Every Saturday morning, everyone writes a note of appreciation to someone for a specific reason.
- Each Sunday night at dinner, everyone discusses how they'll express gratitude and who they'll express it to over the course of the week.[14]

Intentional practice is the starting point for developing intrinsic qualities. When we give opportunities for our children to express gratefulness in tangible ways, the satisfaction that is felt in their hearts creates the desire to cultivate a spirit of gratitude.

Giving without expectation of return creates a sense of gratitude for what might come, not because of an expectation, but from a deep sense of thankfulness.

The Flipside of Gratitude

At Manners of the Heart, we often look at the flipside of issues. For instance, one of our sayings that shows the flipside of respect is that without respect, parents cannot parent, teachers cannot teach, and children cannot learn. To close this chapter, let's briefly look at the flipside of gratitude. Parents are often unaware of the mistakes they make that may lead to ingratitude in their children. These include:

- Not giving opportunities for your children to get outside themselves prevents them from seeing the needs of others.
- Under-parenting through a lack of discipline creates a spoiled child who can't get along with others because they haven't learned how to follow rules.
- Overindulgence shrivels your children's hearts. Just like the Grinch whose heart was two sizes too small when all he could think about was himself, overindulgence drowns your children in stuff, so they behave as if they are entitled to special treatment.

How do you undo the damage done? Use difficult circumstances as teachable moments. Take to heart the suggestions in this chapter, for just as the building of self-respect begins with respecting others, so instilling a heart of gratitude begins with giving, not receiving—learning to live with open hands and open hearts.

All ages can participate in volunteer projects. Tykes, ages three to six, can accompany you to a nursing home or offer a smile when delivering meals to those who are homebound. Tweens can help bag toiletries for the homeless shelter in your community and serve alongside you on the food line. Teens can be a buddy to children in a head start program, perform music in a nursing home, or volunteer to coach on a little league team.

Toys for Tots is an outstanding opportunity for all ages to serve during the holidays. Look around, the needs are great; the opportunities to serve are endless.

Many years ago, following a study of the Good Samaritan parable, small group leader Victoria Fuller gave each participant in her study group a $5 bill and a challenge: "Apply what you've learned by investing the money in someone else."

The only rule was that the beneficiary was not to be anyone they knew well because the man helped by the Good Samaritan was a stranger to him.

Two weeks later, the stories coming back were amazing. One member of her group followed an elderly lady out of the pharmacy after hearing her say she could not afford her prescription. He gave her the money to cover the cost. Several members pooled their money and added more to offer a young couple a night out with free babysitting. Another bought diapers for a single dad who was struggling to make ends meet.[15]

You could do the same with your family. Give each member of the family a few dollars with a challenge to watch and listen for a need they could meet. What a beautiful way to train your children to watch for the needs of others with open hands and open hearts.

To close this chapter, allow me to offer a revolutionary idea to discourage others from throwing trinkets at your children. From television commercials, well-meaning grandparents (just stepped on my own toes), dentist offices, bakery counters, schools, and in a myriad of other places, your children are confronted with "happies" at every turn.

A young dad expressed his angst about this: "What will it take to make it all stop? Everywhere we go, someone is giving our kids candy and trinkets. They don't need the candy, and they don't appreciate the trinkets."

Why not teach your children to say, "No, thank you, I have plenty," or "No, thank you, I have enough," as a response to the offer of a trinket? Now, you're getting serious about changing not only the hearts of your children but shifting the hearts of an entire generation from ingratitude to gratitude.

CHAPTER FIVE

Foster Humility *and* Confidence

STRONG, adj. *Ardent; eager; zealous; earnestly engaged; as a strong partisan.*[1]

Since the early days of writing this book, I have been asking parents which of the three heart attributes they believe to be the most important to instill in their children: humility, respect, or resiliency. In the multitude of answers to date, less than 3 percent have said humility. In fact, it seemed for most, humility wasn't even a consideration, except for one very wise mom.

Our wise mom is the mother of four children, ages eleven to twenty-four. Her older children are kindhearted, good citizens who are making their way in the world. The younger siblings are still under her tutelage, doing well in school, and interested in sports and business. In fact, the youngest of her lot has aspirations of being a business owner one day.

When I asked which of the three attributes she felt was most important, she responded without hesitation, "Humility, because humility is the foundation of respect and resiliency. Without humility, there is no basis for respect. Without humility, when you fail, you give up in defeat."

At the time of our first conversation, I didn't know her husband was a community figure who had recently won election to a new position. In a four-candidate race that many said would be close, he walked away with more than 60 percent of the vote. As the wife of a politician, she brings an interesting perspective to the introduction of humility, since we don't often think of politics as a profession known for humility—even though politicians are meant to be public *servants*.

As running for political office was designed to be, a person throws their hat in the ring because there is a deep-seated belief, based on their experience and wisdom, that they can meet the needs of their constituents through competent, selfless service.

After getting to know this wise woman's husband, I can testify that he, indeed, exudes humility as a confident man who can ask for your vote without shame because he knows his heart. He has proven in the congruency of his words and actions that he is a man of integrity who can lead the residents of his community to a better standard of living.

Within this public servant's story, we find our working definition for humility: being the best you can be for the service of others. Not thinking of what is best for you, but what is best for everyone; using your talents and abilities for the good of all. Humility as an attitude of the heart reveals the answer to the question of why we do what we do. Is it to serve others or to serve self?

In our self-esteem-obsessed culture, many have made humility a sign of weakness, rather than a sign of strength. Self-forgetfulness is the antithesis of the world's viewpoint. Mother Teresa saw humility in the light of truth, when she explained, "If you are humble, nothing will touch you, neither praise nor disgrace, because you know what you are."[2] I would add, you know *why* you are.

A humble child is not a doormat. Quite the contrary, the person who chooses to walk in deference to others stands taller than the rest, as evidenced in our humble politician. It wouldn't surprise me if he lost more races than he won, but his humility and confidence that he has what it takes to help others (humble confidence), keeps him coming back to run again.

The truth is, humble people are the strongest of us all, which should propel us to replace a quest for our children's happiness with an aspiration for their humbleness.

For a fuller understanding, let's look at "a very humble man, more humble than anyone else on the face of the earth" (Num. 12:3).

The Humility of Moses

Moses was written about extensively in the Old Testament and in historical documents of the Israelites. Considered a leader of all leaders, Moses led his people out of Egyptian captivity. As God's messenger, he delivered the Ten Commandments to the world from Mount Sinai.

And yet, the Bible tells us Moses was the humblest man on earth!

Obviously, there's something about humility we have missed in our modern-day definition and understanding of the word. The *Oxford Dictionary* defines humility as, "a modest or low view of one's own importance; humbleness."[3]

In giving further explanation of humility, *Merriam-Webster* adds, "if you describe yourself as 'but a humble editor' or refer to your home as your 'humble abode,' you are saying that neither you nor your home is very impressive."[4] Seems to me we have a disconnect here between the truth and our interpretation of humility.

The explanation for why a man who stood taller than the rest, who was revered for his wisdom, and who commanded the respect of his people was considered the humblest man on earth is found in the etymology of the word.

"Humility is not what it is sometimes taken to be—a low estimate of oneself. That is false or counterfeit humility. True humility is mindlessness of self,"[5] Rabbi Jonathan Sacks explains.

The word humility has two interesting roots. The first comes from the Hebrew word *anavah*, which means, "to occupy your God-given space in the world—to not overestimate yourself or your abilities, but to not underestimate them either."[6]

As Dave Adamson points out, "*Anavah* is being aware of and comfortable with your place. . . . We don't take up so much space that it squeezes others out, and we don't take up so little space that our responsibilities fall to others."[7]

Or, in other words, a humble person doesn't bother to think about himself because he has more important things to think about, as in Moses' case.

Translated from the Latin, the second meaning of humility comes from *humus*, which is the earth. How interesting to put the two together for a deeper understanding of humility—to stand your ground in your God-given space having fully cultivated your talents and abilities for the good of others. This is the humility I want to help you foster in your children.

My husband's definition of humility adds another dimension: "A humble person is satisfied where they are, so they can put the needs of others ahead of themselves. They're in a good place with God."

No doubt, Moses was a man in a good place with God.

Humble Confidence

Look back at the wise mom's comment from the opening of this chapter: "*Without* humility, when you fail, you give up in defeat." An arrogant person fights back in the face of defeat and learns nothing from the failure. A humble person accepts the defeat, examines the errors made, looks for ways in which to improve, and comes out a better person who is better able to serve. Humble people have the ability to accept defeat and try again, which will inevitably lead to victory.

A humble person is a peacemaker, a trusted friend, a leader of leaders, not easily intimidated, a StrongHeart.

Industrialist and physician Armand Hammer once said, "A person starts to live when he can live outside himself."[8] Do you see that humility and confidence are not opposites, but flow one from the other? They are not diametrically opposed. The messages of our culture tell our children that they have to fight, compete, and perform to have self-worth. Our culture preaches the "me" doctrine. Do whatever it takes to be number one. You're nobody unless you're somebody.

Instead, truth says if you are fostering humility in your children, they won't be easily distracted or discouraged. They will be confident in who they are and whose they are. They will know they have a purpose that will bring satisfaction far beyond anything the world has to offer. They will look beyond themselves to find satisfaction, not in what they get, but in what they give. This is one of the foundational attributes of a StrongHeart.

Raising children with humble confidence begins with understanding:

- We were put here to serve, not to be served.
- It is more important what we give the world, than what the world gives us.
- The reasons *why* we do what we do are more important than what we do.
- It is through true humility that we gain confidence.

Your children's confidence comes in finding meaningful ways they can contribute to the lives of others. While telling a four-year-old she did a great job on her artwork will encourage her, helping her know her artwork made someone smile when they saw it can reveal a deeper level of meaning to her work. A ten-year-old will enjoy hearing that he is special, but he also needs to know his kindness toward his younger brother is appreciated.

We can help our children develop humble confidence by encouraging them to be the best they can be. Not pushing them to be number one, but to work hard with their abilities. When children develop their talents, they discover how much they have to contribute to the world.

In our elementary school work, we don't offer incentives but a much greater motivation—the inspiration of working hard so our students experience the satisfaction of helping someone else learn what they have mastered. Rather than looking for a trophy, Manners of the Heart kids look for how they can take the knowledge they've gained and use it to help a classmate who is struggling. They say thank you when the spotlight is on them, and then step aside so the light shines behind them for others to find their way.

In fostering humble confidence, working on the attitude behind the action makes the difference. Rather than focus on the external action, look for the internal motivation that will reveal the presence or absence of humility.

Looking at why an action is done calls into play the "So That's." Here are a few ways to foster humble confidence using the "So That's":

- When asking your child to dig into homework, connect the request to how it will affect others. You can say:
  - "Let's practice these math problems *so that* you can master them and help someone else."
  - "Work hard to develop your writing skills *so that* you can write words that inspire others."
- When asking your child to take care of their things, connect the request to how it will affect others. You can say:
  - "Let's take care of our library books *so that* they will be available for other kids to use."

  - "Let's pick up these shoes in the middle of your room *so that* no one comes in and trips over them."
- When your child "gets it," you can say:
  - "Wow, you are so blessed to be able help a classmate, friend, or sibling who is struggling to learn how to ________________."
  - "I know you are excited you've learned to play the guitar, and I am too. I know it's taken a lot of hard work. Why don't you introduce your friend to the guitar and ask if they would like to learn? They might enjoy learning from you."

If we want our children to experience life to the fullest, to become all God created them to be, we must instill the understanding that true humility is being your best *so that* you can help others become their best. We must help our children discover their gifts and abilities so that they can be developed and shared with the world. That's what brings true happiness—joy.

If you made a commitment in the last chapter to implement chores, you're already fostering humble confidence in your children. If not, let me convince you to start today!

Life Skills in the Making

Self-worth is developed in children when they contribute to the well-being of the family by doing chores. When my husband left his family behind, our twelve-year-old sons, who had been raised doing chores, naturally stepped up to help me. Their responsibilities had given them confidence to help in a time of need.

Doing laundry, helping with meal prep, running a vacuum cleaner, and cutting the grass were nothing out of the ordinary. As a matter of fact, the boys didn't need a lot of prodding because the remarkable by-product of doing chores is the development of self-respect. Pitching in to help "just because" is the greatest of all internal motivators.

As my sons entered high school, I had something akin to a panic attack when I realized I only had four more years to train them in all they needed to survive on their own. I made a list of survival skills that looked something like this:

1. Food planning/shopping/preparation (we had started cooking together when they were six)
2. Kitchen cleaning (got this)
3. Cleaning bathroom (got this)
4. Laundry details (got this)
5. Budgeting/paying bills/keeping checking account records (Christmas saving accounts helped)
6. Organizing workspace (needs work)
7. Change a tire/car maintenance
8. Emergency situations (car trouble, car wreck, etc.)
9. Job skills/interviewing/expectations

After completing the list, I realized the skills they needed for living on their own were grounded in the chores they had learned in elementary and middle school. In addition, just as I had learned a strong work ethic from my parents, my hope was that my sons had witnessed the same commitment to hard work in their dad and me. I was confident they were now ready to take on more complex tasks because of the experience and knowledge they had gained from simple assignments in their younger years.

When my sons entered college, they were the only freshmen (male or female) in their group of friends who knew how to prepare a three-course meal and clean a bathroom. When teased by their buddies for being good "housekeepers," they usually replied, "You just wish you knew how to do this stuff, 'cause it makes life easier."

Character-Building Confidence

Chores are not only habit-forming, but character-building. In a study out of the University of Minnesota, Marty Rossman, professor emeritus, found that "young adults who began chores at ages 3 and 4 were more likely to have good relationships with family and friends, to achieve academic and early career success and to be self-sufficient, as compared with those who didn't have chores or who started them as teens." Giving children household chores at an early age helps to build a lasting sense of mastery, responsibility, and self-reliance.[9]

As your children become adept at taking care of their chores, life skills are developed that will serve them well later in life. Humility balanced with confidence in their abilities equips them to excel in all areas of life. Rather than compete with others, they compete with themselves and cooperate with others. A proud dad shared a special moment that happened with his sixteen-year-old son following a horrific storm that ravaged their community many years ago.

From Chores to Volunteer to Career

Darius (fictitious name) shared at the supper table one night that he had volunteered to be part of a team to help clean up homes of families in need. When his dad asked his son about his decision, his son replied, "Dad, I knew I could help because I've been helping out around here since I was a little kid. I knew that I knew enough about fixing things in a house to help somebody else."

For the next six months, the eager teenager spent Saturdays and Sunday afternoons serving on volunteer work crews. When summer rolled around, he got a job in construction work. He's now made a decision to study construction management in college. He feels a strong pull to disaster relief projects and even wonders if there's a better way to rebuild after a catastrophe. It won't surprise me if one day he conceives of a breakthrough plan that changes the way we serve those in time of need.

One of the greatest joys as a parent is to witness your child helping others without thought of "what's in it for me."

Living to serve.

Humble Confidence on and off the Field

Humility—true humility—is one of the most expansive and life-enhancing of all virtues. It does not mean undervaluing yourself. It means valuing other people.[10]

John loves playing soccer. He trains, studies, and plays hard, on the field and off. He spends time with friends, while maintaining a strong work ethic. He finds a healthy balance in his life that enables him to perform at a high level of excellence for all the right reasons.

John's coach says he has extraordinary talent, but his strongest quality is that he is teachable. With his "right" attitude, he has the potential to play well beyond high school. He has confidence in his coach, confidence in his teammates, and confidence in his abilities, but humility in his heart. He is determined to use his talent to the fullest because he wants to find out how far he can go and who he can take with him.

John's leadership skills are showing on the field, as he leads his team to consistent wins. He's also leading as a valuable member of the student council.

A mom of a tween daughter and a teen son shared these thoughts on humble confidence:

> Your purpose always involves serving others, the good of humanity, a reason for being here that far outlives your time on earth. What you leave behind is dependent on your humble confidence.
>
> Humble confidence allows you to be free to be who God designed you to be. You have no agenda of your own. Your deepest

> desire is to discover God's will for your life and spend your life fulfilling it for His glory, not your own.
>
> Humble confidence is living with purpose. Not living for yourself, but for the good of others. Nothing feels as good as a job well done that helped someone else.[11]

Danny Huerta, vice president of Parenting and Youth at Focus on the Family, adds, "Opportunities to engage and serve others are embraced as invitations rather than dreaded as inconveniences to a humble teen."[12] Rather than spending their days looking for others to serve them, they find great joy in serving others. When they enter the workforce, they make better employees because they understand no one will do their work for them. They're the ones who pitch in when someone needs help.

The fostering of humble confidence in your child enables the development of guts, resiliency, tenacity, and integrity from a foundation of true strength.

Be an Example of Humble Confldence

You are your children's greatest and most infiuential teacher. Here are a few ways to show them what humble confidence looks like:

- Speaking well of others and congratulating them for a job well done
- Giving credit where credit is due
- Performing kindnesses for others without recognition
- Being patient with others
- Apologizing when at fault and seeking forgiveness

CHAPTER SIX

Encourage Bravery

STRONG, adj. *Having virtues of great efficacy; or having a particular quality in a great degree.*[1]

For the past three years, I've been asking people, "What comes to your mind when you hear the term StrongHeart?" More times than I can count, the answer has been *Braveheart*, a 1995 film loosely based on the Scottish hero William Wallace. (I was delighted that *Braveheart*, my all-time favorite movie, came to the mind of so many people.)

Here are the top six answers to "Why *Braveheart*?"

- The main character had a strong heart.
- He was a leader.
- He had courage.
- He was a man on a mission. He had a purpose.
- He was the most passionate leader I've ever seen.
- He didn't give up when he was betrayed.

When *Braveheart* was released in 1995, my sons were in middle school. Even though it had been given an "R" rating (an "R" rating twenty-five years ago was quite different than an "R" rating today), when the boys turned sixteen, we watched it together. As a result of the movie, a deep conversation about bravery continued throughout their high school years.

My sons came to believe that bravery is standing up for the right against the wrong because you know who you are and what you stand for.

While we know some of the historical details of *Braveheart* were not accurate, the portrayal of the courage and conviction of Wallace, the thirteenth-century Scottish freedom fighter, has never been in dispute. He was, as the movie depicted, filled with integrity and tenacity. For many reasons, William Wallace is the epitome of bravery, as I define it for you and your children:

- He was insulated with truth.
- He fought for something bigger than himself.
- He did it afraid.
- He had moral courage that undergirded his bravery.

I urge you to watch *Braveheart* as parents who want to parent well.* Watch as parents who want to raise StrongHearts who will possess moral courage that enables them to live bravely when faced with trials and temptations. StrongHearts who will lead their peers through the cultural battles of their generation.

Let me warn you, I had many friends who could not believe I was such a fan of the movie because of the graphic battle scenes between the Scots and the English. I believed then, as I do now—war is ugly. It is brutal. At times, it is necessary. The battle William Wallace fought for his people seven hundred years ago was intense, but no more so than the battle raging for the souls of our children today.

How do we begin to encourage the bravery of William Wallace in our children? It begins with grounding them in truth, so they know what they believe and what they stand for.

* To find a *Braveheart* viewing guide with discussion questions for parents, visit jillgarnercontent .org/movies.

Insulate Their Hearts with Truth

One of my ten-year-old sons stood in front of me after being caught in a lie. He knew it, but his body language made it clear he was going to attempt to convince me otherwise. To keep him from digging a deeper hole, I leaned down, looked him directly in his eyes, and said, "Whatever is getting ready to come out of your mouth better be the absolute truth. Anything less than the absolute truth, and your discipline will be double the discipline for the crime committed."

I didn't move. He didn't move. I waited. Finally, the truth came pouring out.

I thanked him for being truthful and rendered the appropriate discipline for the misdeed that had led to his lying. Children need to know we all make mistakes, but lying about our mistakes is worse than the mistake.

Insulating Your Young Children's Hearts

Instilling the importance of honesty in our children helps them understand there is a standard of truth to be upheld. Here are a few thoughts on laying a foundation of truth in your home and in your young child's heart:

- Be careful of the words you speak. No stretching the truth (still lying), no exaggerating (still lying), no saying one thing and doing another (dishonest), no breaking promises (lying). You can introduce your children to the concept of absolute truth at an early age, when you don't bend the rules or gloss over "little white lies."
- As we discussed in chapter 2, giving false praise to your child is lying. Your child needs to know you will always tell them the truth, even when it is hard. They learn from you that flattery is

lying and hurts the one receiving it. They also learn how to speak the truth in love.

- There should always be a consequence for even the tiniest lie. I know it's cute when a preschooler "fibs." But remember one lie, unchecked, always leads to another. If positive attention is gained from one lie, another will follow, and then another. Three is a magic number with children. Three times for anything and a pattern of behavior is set in place that will have to be undone.

It is our responsibility to nurture our young children in being truth tellers, so they will become truth seekers in their teen years.

Insulating Your Teens' Hearts

As your children mature, they will be confronted with relativism, the idea there is no such thing as absolute truth. That each of us has our own truth, according to our own beliefs. That there is no universal standard for truth, which is absolutely *not* true!

In a recent Barna Research study, adults and teens were asked their beliefs on the unchanging truth of moral absolutes. The study further asked the question of whether moral truth is relative to circumstances. The startling finding was that 64 percent of adults consider truth relative to the person and their situation. The percentage of teenagers who believe moral truth is relative to circumstances far surpassed the adults at 83 percent. Sadly, only 6 percent of teenagers surveyed said moral truth is absolute.[2]

Growing up in our entitled society, teenagers were quick to respond that they looked for the greatest personal benefits in making their moral choices at an alarming rate of one out of six. The study identified three alternative foundations by one out of ten teens—"whatever would make the most people happy, whatever they thought their family and friends expected of them, and on the basis of the values taught by their parents."[3]

According to Dr. George Barna, "Americans have historically held the biblical view that God created our world and the life within it, and He gave specific guidelines that promote our well-being when we stay within those boundaries. Those principles were delivered to humanity through the Bible." Whether all Americans believed in God as Creator, the principles presented in the Bible were considered "consistent and pertinent to everyone, in all situations, at all times."[4]

Today, most Americans are defining their life purpose apart from the intent of God. As Dr. Barna explained, "Now we see that Americans have rejected the idea that God is truth and that the truth principles He has given for our good are reliable and relevant. We trust ourselves or our discoveries rather than the truth principles God provides."[5]

Yes, it seems truth has been buried beneath piles of trash in the scrapyard of our country's ever digressing culture. Truth has become as worthless as an old sterling silver serving piece that was once considered a prized possession to be held in high regard but is now sold off for pennies. Beautiful silver pieces are now found at the bottom of the trash heap, discarded, tarnished, and forgotten, just as truth is, because no value is placed in either.

It is our duty to reawaken truth in our culture for the sake of our children and the next generation.

It is our duty to reawaken truth in our culture for the sake of our children and the next generation. We must be vigilant in insulating the hearts of our children with truth, timeless truth, that will protect them from falling prey to the lies of our culture.

The truth is . . . there is absolute truth—truth that is true for all people, for all places, and for all time. Out of that truth are born principles for moral living. Murder is wrong. Cheating is wrong. Deceit is wrong. Stealing is wrong. We would never encourage children to murder, cheat, deceive, or steal because these behaviors are absolutely wrong. Whether we accept the principles laid forth in the Ten Commandants, they are the foundation of a civil society. When followed, the wisdom presented in the book of Proverbs leads to a good life. When these are replaced with whatever feels good, whatever makes you happy, and whatever you want, nothing but misery will follow. Escalation in the grim statistics of suicide, drug addiction, depression, and anxiety among our teenagers and young adults prove the truth of this statement.

Instilling the importance of absolute truth in our teens helps them understand there is a standard of truth to be upheld. Here are a few thoughts on how to build on the foundation of truth already laid in your teen's heart:

- Remind your teen that bad company rubs off on them. Help your teen understand the importance of the friends they keep. Hanging out with friends who use profanity will cause them to buy into it. Without being aware, they will be conditioned to use that same language. Unconscious of their words, profanity will fall out of their mouths without warning.
- Remind your teen that borrowing others' belongings without permission is stealing. Not returning money borrowed or not returning an item loaned, is just as dishonest as stealing.
- Not being truthful with friends, even in the tiniest of details, hurts relationships. It's difficult to regain the trust of a friend if you've ever been dishonest with them.
- Keep your promises to your teen. Breaking your word is just as much a lie, as your teen breaking their promise to you. Don't make a promise in the first place that will be impossible to keep. Encourage your teen to be thoughtful when making promises to others.

Establishing a standard of truth in your home sets the stage for encouraging bravery. Truth builds trust that enables your children to see beyond themselves to a higher purpose that will call for bravery.

A Purpose Bigger Than Themselves

You may have read a part of this story in one of my earlier books, but it bears repeating.[6]

Tears still come to my eyes when I think of a young soldier with whom I visited in the Atlanta airport during a four-hour delay. He was heading out for his third tour in Afghanistan as a combatant.

He was open and respectful of my unending questions. He answered with honesty and sincerity as I asked about his family, what led him to the military, and then finally, the gnawing question: "What do you think about when you face down the enemy?"

With great humility and seriousness, he replied, "I'm thinking about my momma, my sister, and all the folks at home."

I swallowed hard, and asked, "Are you afraid of dying?"

Without hesitation, he answered, "No, ma'am. I'm more afraid of *failing* than dying. Because if I fail, *somebody else* might die."

Our eyes had been locked, until that statement. With grasped hands and forearms resting on his thighs, he lowered his head for his own tears to fall away. I reached over to rub his back.

In this sacred moment, time stood still.

The bravery of this young man to fight, not for himself but for others, was inspiring, and still is. To fight for his family, for his countrymen, for freedom. I doubt he would have had the same resolve if he were only thinking of himself.

He had shared he was in trouble a lot as a kid. He had been labeled as a strong-willed child in kindergarten. But his personal assessment of himself was that he was selfish and spoiled. He signed up for military service because he recognized he wasn't going to get anywhere in life without self-discipline, and he figured the military "would whip him into shape."

What he found was a purpose beyond himself. A reason to give his best. A reason to become more than what he was.

Helping Your Children See Beyond Themselves

We're going to go deeper with helping your children see beyond themselves in chapter 8 when we discuss others-centeredness, but for now consider the following points.

We don't give incentives in our elementary curriculum; we inspire children to do the right thing. We don't use stickers or treats or trinkets because we give them something else to aspire to that's bigger than themselves.

We see this desperate cry for something more in today's teens and young adults who grew up being told life was all about them. Doing whatever it takes to get in the "right" college. Taking in all the world has to offer. Wearing the "right" clothes. Becoming social media darlings. And on and on . . .

All the while we fed their self-esteem, we did little to help them develop self-respect, which comes from contributing to the world around them, from finding a purpose beyond the "stuff" the world offers. In many ways, we drain our children's souls rather than fill them when we make life about what they will do one day rather than who they will become.

A great exercise for instilling the understanding of seeing beyond yourself in your children is working a jigsaw puzzle. The whole family can get involved. Here are a few teaching points to use as you're working the puzzle:

1. Life is like a giant puzzle, and each of us is a piece of the puzzle.
2. The maker of the puzzle designed and manufactured it so that each piece fits into one predetermined spot.
3. The final puzzle will be just as he designed it to be.
4. As we each find our spot in the puzzle, we enable others to find their spot.
5. There must be interdependence of the pieces to complete the puzzle.
6. If one piece is missing, the puzzle cannot be completed.

This is a wonderful way of helping your children understand they have an important part to play in God's plan for the world. Just as William Wallace understood the role he was to play in his people gaining freedom, each of us has an important role to play in helping others find their place. When it's your children's turn to step up, it will take the ability to see beyond themselves to the greater good to take that step, even though they will be afraid to do it.

Just Do It Afraid

When I was a child, I was afraid of water, dogs, heights, people, and, worst of all, the dark. My inordinate fear of the dark came from watching an after-school TV show, *Dark Shadows*. I was much too young to process it. (Note: Be careful of what you allow your young children to watch. Once children see certain images, especially disturbing ones, it can be extremely difficult for young minds to forget them.)

As it turned out, many of my fears were instilled in me by my mother, who was terrified of dogs, horrified of the water, and petrified of heights. She didn't realize she was passing those fears on to me by not facing them in herself.

In my elementary years, I wrecked more than one or two outings with panic attacks, crying, and pleading to go home as an anxious little girl who had not been equipped to overcome my fears.

In high school, any sudden change of plans brought anxiety that presented as stomachaches or headaches. I missed more events than I attended, due to the fear of something. I learned the hard way that focusing on the problem rather than the solution only made the problem worse. When a trusted family friend wisely suggested rather than trying to get rid of the fear of people, use the fear to my advantage, things began to change. My infamous "butterflies" that led to a debilitating stomachache were used as an extra dose of energy to "carry" me onstage before a large crowd. The fear of heights was met head-on the day I was pressured to navigate a high-ropes course tethered to links and ropes, which prevented the underlying fear of falling. Looking down on the world from the top of a tree gave me a new perspective on overcoming fear.

Looking for ways to help your children overcome their fears?

- Try using "I'm afraid, but . . ." with your children when a fear has taken control of them, so they can learn how to take control of the fear themselves. You'll be teaching them that they lose out when they allow fear to win. It works like this:
  - If they're afraid of heights and their friends are going to a rock-climbing wall, suggest for thought: *I'm afraid, but if I don't try, I'll miss out on a great adventure with my friends and finding out how good it feels to not let fear stop me.*
  - If they're afraid of water and their friends are heading to the water park, suggest for thought: *I'm afraid, but if I don't try, I'll miss out on all the fun of getting in line with my friends and gliding down the big slide at the water park and finding out how good it feels to not let fear stop me.*

- If they're afraid of speaking in front of people, suggest this thought: *I'm afraid, but if I don't try, I'll never know if I can do it and find out how good it feels to not let fear stop me.*

In addition to "I'm afraid, but . . ." here are a few more ways to help your children overcome their fears:

- Listen with your eyes, your ears, and your heart. Allow your child to share their fear without criticism or dismissal. Don't make too much of the fear, but don't make too little of it either. Equip your child with the three As of fear as more than a coping mechanism, as a way to keep him from being defeated by the fear:
  - Acknowledge the fear/Admit you're afraid
  - Ask "what if" questions/Ask what's the worst that could happen?
  - Act on it/Move forward into action. Don't allow the fear to paralyze you.
- Share a story of a time you were afraid and how you overcame your fear.
- Use books to help your child overcome her fears:
  - *I'm a Scaredy Cat* is a delightful book that gives children the reassurance that they're not alone when they're afraid.[7]
  - *God Is Bigger Than That* lets children know, no matter what they face, God is bigger than their fears.[8]
  - *It Will Be Okay* teaches children that new circumstances may cause fear, but they don't have to be afraid.[9]
- Memorizing a few Bible verses about fear strengthens a child's resolve to do it afraid:
  - "Be strong and courageous. Do not be afraid, for the Lord your God is with you wherever you go." (Josh. 1:9)
  - "I sought the Lord, and he answered me and delivered me from all my fears." (Ps. 34:4)
  - "When I am afraid, I put my trust in you." (Ps. 56:3)

Every time your child pushes fear aside to try something new, remind them their fears diminish with each triumph, just as their hearts grow stronger with each right decision. With each personal victory, they gain confidence to be even braver in the next challenge. Nothing instills courage the way a victory does.

When I became a mother, I was determined I wouldn't pass along to my sons the fears of childhood I had worked hard to overcome. My goal was to help my sons develop courage in their hearts so they could be brave in their actions. We often reminded ourselves that "scared is what you're feeling but brave is what you're doing."

Physical Courage to Take the Jump

To begin the process of developing courage, we need to go back to one of the soul questions in the the "Home of Respect" chart: Who do I belong to? We satisfy this question by offering recognition, paying attention when they need us most, and showing ownership as our beloved children; all of which builds security that leads to bravery.

For most of us, jumping in the swimming pool was our first memory of mustering up courage. The scene probably went something like this:

> "Jump, honey, jump," Daddy urged as he stood in chest deep water, while his little girl perched on the side of the pool tries to muster up enough courage in her heart to take the plunge. "You can do it! You can do it! JUUUMMMMP!" Daddy insisted. And with his extra reassurance, his terrified little girl put aside her fear and jumped, landing in the arms of her daddy.

Would she have jumped without her daddy's arms awaiting her? Maybe later in life, but not this day. Knowing she was not alone in her risk-taking encouraged her to take the jump, despite her fear. After a few jumps, she was ready for Daddy to sit on the side of the pool and watch.

When our children know we are there for them, they have the security to jump outside their comfort zone.

Knowing to whom they belong encourages children to muster the physical courage to jump into challenges. One of the dads I interviewed for the book said, "In relationship with 'doing hard things,' it is natural to experience apprehension. I remind our kids that the same emotion that is called 'fear' is also called 'anticipation.' It's a matter of how we frame the issue of the unknown 'thing' that is before us."[10]

Stepping Outside Their Comfort Zone

Several years ago, a friend started taking her four-year-old daughter, Haley, to visit her great-grandmother in a nursing home. Haley was reluctant at first, not wanting to talk to anyone. She didn't want to go back after the first visit, so my wise friend used a bit of persuasive pressure by suggesting they could make Haley's favorite cookies to take on their next visit.

Haley couldn't wait to get out of the car for the second visit because she loved sharing her baked treats. She quickly warmed up to the gentle voices and sweet comments from the residents about her delicious cookies and looked forward to returning.

Wednesdays for lunch became their regular routine. Haley learned to play checkers and loved sharing her artwork with her special friends.

Fast-forward. Today, Haley is a young professional who sets aside time each week to volunteer. When asked about her love of volunteering, she credits her mom for giving her the courage as a little girl to be brave enough to reach out.

Here are other ways to help your children go beyond their comfort zone:

- Ask your child about their hero. Then ask why they view that person as a hero. You will be able to help your child see the admirable qualities they can emulate.
- Encourage your child to ask questions by asking questions yourself. Let your children see you go out of your comfort zone. Talking to the cashier at the grocery. Helping a neighbor in need. Standing up for your beliefs.
- When my granddaughters were apprehensive about their new classrooms, we made a batch of homemade cookies for their classmates. On the first day of class, the girls walked into their classes with a basket of cookies to share. This simple act relieved their anxiety of a new place and enabled them to meet everyone quickly.
- Before the school day begins, encourage your child to look for someone new to speak to at school. At the end of the day, ask if they met anyone new that day.
- Encourage your child to try new things, such as joining a team or after school club, or taking music lessons. Point out that it's the first step that is the hardest.
- Remind your child of what they will miss if they don't join in. It's more fun to be a part of the fun than to watch the fun.
- Expect your child to admit when they forget their homework or make a mistake rather than trying to hide it or work around it.
- Give your child opportunities to serve in small ways. Pick up the newspaper in a neighbor's front yard and leave it on their doorstep.
- Show your child how to do a new skill. Work with them and then allow them to experience the process of trial and error to build their confidence.

- With tykes, be careful about giving in to picky eaters. Encourage children to try new foods before they're given their standard fare. As silly as it sounds, you will help them build courage to try new things later in life.

Grounded in Moral Courage

Knowing what they stand for grounds your children in moral courage. In the classic *To Kill a Mockingbird*, Atticus Finch explains courage to his son, Jem: "Real courage is when you know you're licked before you begin but you begin anyway, and you see it through no matter what."[11] It's moral courage that gives the fortitude to stick it out to the end.

The root of courage is *cor*, which is Latin for heart.[12] In its original form, courage is "the quality of heart that enables a person to face difficulty, danger, pain, in spite of fear."[13] Another dictionary states, "the ability to overcome one's fear, do or live things which one finds frightening."[14] And one more, "the ability to maintain one's will or intent despite either the experience of fear, frailty or frustration, or the occurrence of adversity, difficulty, defeat, or reversal. Moral fortitude."[15]

In the world your children are entering, moral courage (moral fortitude), is an indispensable heart attribute. If we want our children to be able to do what they know in their hearts is the right thing to do, even if no one does it with them; if we want our children to be able to say what they know are the right words to say, even if no one agrees with them; we must instill core beliefs on which they can stand.

Let me encourage you to set aside some time to formulate your family's core beliefs on which your children develop moral courage. The Stern family has done just that with their Family Life Guides. Words from the guides are painted on a sign in the main hallway of Jason and Andrea Stern's home:

LOVE JESUS. LOVE PEOPLE.

Put on the garment of praise.

It is NEVER necessary to be UNKIND.

Fear is a LIAR.

DO RIGHT

SMILE

Try new things

LOOK for ways to bless

ASSUME THE BEST

In explaining their Family Life Guides, Jason said:

> When we remember to "Love Jesus. Love People," we keep ourselves servant hearted. These family guides help us point back to Jesus who has entrusted us with His Truth, His Gospel, His Love—all things we don't deserve, but have been gifted. What a glorious treasure! Treasuring those thoughts is a way for us to tap into the moral courage to walk out these guides (truths) in our lives, laying down our pride and "rights," and taking up vulnerability and peaceful servants' hearts.[16]

Children who have been grounded in absolute truth within a family structure held together with core beliefs are prepared to do battle from a place of great strength of character. Morally courageous children will stand up for what is right, defend the helpless, and resist peer pressure.

The reason so many children and teens today fall prey to the lies of our culture is because they are not grounded in truth. They don't have a why behind their decisions, only feelings. They have nothing to stand on or hold on to when faced with peer pressure. The winds of our culture blow them over because they have no stake in the ground to give them stability.

Scaredy-Cat Turned Hero

When Dorothy first met the scaredy-cat lion in *The Wizard of Oz*, she snapped, "Why, you're nothing but a big coward." He responded with tears in his eyes, "You're right. I am a coward. I haven't any courage at all."

The Cowardly Lion was even afraid of the sheep he counted when he tried to sleep, until Dorothy needed protection from the Wicked Witch's guards. The lion loudly proclaimed, "Which one of you first? I'll fight you both together if you want. I'll fight you with one paw tied behind my back. I'll fight you standing on one foot. I'll fight you with my eyes closed."[17] When his friend needed protection, the moral courage he possessed propelled him to be brave. In that moment, the cowardly lion learned what Mark Twain knew, "Courage is resistance to fear, mastery of fear—not absence of fear."[18]

Brave Hero, One and the Same

Another well-known character who is mentioned frequently in reference to "StrongHeart" is David from the Bible. Interestingly, most folks who mentioned David said *King* David. But long before David became a powerful king, he developed moral courage as a boy at the feet of his father and in the pasture tending sheep.

The story of David and Goliath is one of the best-known stories in and out of the Bible. Children and adults love the story of the teenage boy who slew the giant that grown men were too afraid to take on. Most often the story is told as a little guy standing against a giant of a man. But I'd like to flip that narrative. I believe the truth is that the one who didn't stand a chance was not David, but Goliath. Let's take a closer look.

David, a Prepared Hero

The nation of Israel was called to fight the Philistine army on opposite sides of the Valley of Elah. David's brothers were sent to the battlefield, but David, the youngest of Jesse's twelve sons, was not old enough to join the army and stayed behind to tend sheep.

One fateful day, Jesse sent David to the battlefield to take provisions to his brothers. When he arrived, the nine-foot-tall Goliath was standing in defiance of the armies of Israel, as he had for forty days and forty nights without opposition.

Rather than run away in fear, teenaged David was ready to jump into action to defend the name of his God and to protect his fellow countrymen.

When David stepped forward, his own brothers mocked him. King Saul balked at him and asked David what credentials he had that would enable him to stand against such a formidable opponent.

David stated his case to King Saul for his worthiness of the task,

> "Your servant has been keeping his father's sheep. When a lion or a bear came and carried off a sheep from the flock, I went after it, struck it, and rescued the sheep from its mouth. When it turned on me, I seized it by its hair, struck it and killed it. . . . The LORD who rescued me from the paw of the lion and the paw of the bear will rescue me from the hand of this Philistine." (1 Sam. 17:34–35, 37)

King Saul accepted David's offer, but not without placing his armor and bronze helmet on him. David placed them on his body but declared they were not for him. Not out of arrogance, but humble confidence. He knew he had all the armor he needed.

David gathered five stones (one for each of the five giants in the Philistine army) because that was all the ammunition he would need (1 Sam. 17:40). Neither Saul, David's brothers, nor Goliath recognized that David was more prepared for battle than any of them, especially Goliath. All they could see was David's outward appearance. They could not see the content of his heart.

Making little of Goliath's weapon, David whirled his slingshot, launching a missile. In one fell swoop, the giant was downed.

Without realizing it, David had been preparing to face whatever giant might come his way in his lifetime. His dedication in tending sheep and his trust in God allowed him to see God's provision for his safety. David knew God would be with him in whatever he was called to do. He knew Goliath was no more a worthy opponent than the lions and bears he had slain in the protection of his sheep.

We make the same mistake as parents that Saul made as king. We try to outfit our children with the trappings of the world, while they're telling us through their behavior that's not what they need. Their deepest need is for us to point them to the source for all their needs—a relationship with Jesus. We are called to help prepare our children with moral courage. But only God can save and secure their souls for eternity.

CHAPTER SEVEN

Develop GRIT (Guts, Resilience, Integrity, Tenacity)

STRONG, adj. *Well established; firm; not easily overthrown or altered; as a custom grown strong by time.*[1]

After too many years of not working out, I decided it was time to get back in shape. My first day at the gym, I met a former weight-lifting champion with a thick European accent, an ominous presence, and a heart of gold. Still pumping iron five days a week, he took pity on this out-of-shape fifty-something-year-old and offered to work with me.

My well-experienced trainer helped me find muscles I didn't know existed. My aching body taught me new lessons in perseverance. He had high expectations and was relentless in pressuring me to achieve more than I believed I could.

Whenever I complained, as a reminder of his commitment to my excellence, he would say, "I'll never lie to you. I'll always tell you the truth. I'll *encourage* you when you *need* it, but I'll *pressure* you when I *know* you need it."

"Persuasive pressure" is what I call my trainer's brand of encouragement. Through his raw honesty, he persuaded me to keep going. Not by making the workouts easy, but by challenging me and then helping me live up to the challenge. And to an even greater degree, living up to the challenge himself.

When I was ready to stop a series of reps before he was ready for me to stop, he would squat near my ear and with that convincing accent, whisper, "Where's your *grrrit*? It takes *grrrit* to try. *Grrrit* to try again. *Grrrit* to learn. *Grrrit* to keep going. Where's your *grrrit*?" With every "grrrit," he added a bit of a fist pump. (I wish you could see his gnarled face, hear his rumbling voice, and feel his passion, as I do while typing this paragraph.) By the conclusion of his monologue on grit, the series of reps he had planned were completed through his persuasive pressure.

Psychologist Angela Lee Duckworth defines grit as "the ability to persevere in pursuing a future goal over a long period of time and not giving up. . . . It is having stamina. It's sticking with your future, day-in, day-out, not just for the week, not just for the month, but for years and working really hard to make that future a reality. Grit is living life like it's a marathon, not a sprint."[2]

It won't surprise you that I like old-fashioned, but not antiquated, words for grit. Sometimes older words paint a clearer picture of a new concept than contemporary words. Try these: Endurance. Stick-to-itiveness. Fortitude. Steadfastness. Determination.

Others have defined grit as:

- The ability to stick to the task at hand no matter the obstacles, until the goal is met.
- Believing there's something more for you than you can see right in front of you.
- Refusing to give up, even when everyone else has given up.

- The relentless resolve to keep pursuing a desired goal and not giving up.[3]

Benjamin Franklin once said, "Think of these things, whence you came, where you are going, and to whom you must account."[4]

My personal favorite definition for grit is "stubbornness with a purpose." I've seen this phrase used to define perseverance or persistence, but I prefer to use it as an explanation of grit. Stubbornness with a purpose defines the process of developing grit. The relentless pursuit of something bigger than we can achieve on our own. The purpose of being a parent is to help our children find their purpose.

I often say we have been given a sacred honor, and therefore a holy duty, to raise His children to become all He created them to be. In other words, to find His purpose for their lives to make sticking with it worth it.

If our deepest desire is to raise StrongHearts who can overcome the distractions, the disappointments, and the disservice of our culture to become all they are meant to be, we must help our children develop GRIT—which stands for Guts, Resilience, Integrity, and Tenacity.

Following my trainer's lead, you can learn to apply "persuasive pressure" with love that will enable your children to meet the challenges of life. Let's take a look at each of these attributes.

G Is for GUTS

The first step in helping our children develop grit is helping them find the guts to try something new, to offer someone their help, to stand up for the right, or even to answer a question in class.

A Reluctant First Grader

Jennifer was a reluctant first grader when it came to trying new things. She didn't like attention and tried to stay out of the limelight, but

Jennifer had a sweet singing voice that others noticed.

When she was chosen to sing a solo in the Christmas pageant, Jennifer begged her mom not to make her sing. She begged her choir director to pick someone else, but the choir director smiled and told her she would do just fine.

After several practices in the choir room, it was time for Jennifer to practice on stage. She muddled through but continued to be terrified of the real performance.

The night of the pageant arrived. All was going well, until it was Jennifer's turn to step to the microphone. She froze, staring into the audience with glassy eyes. Everyone waited. After a long, uncomfortable silence, Jennifer's mom, who couldn't carry a tune, stood, and terribly off-key, sang, "Away in a manger, no crib for a bed" to encourage her daughter.

When Jennifer saw her mother's willingness to try to do something she knew she couldn't do, for her sake, Jennifer took over from the stage and finished the carol to the audience's delight.

Can you imagine Jennifer never needing prodding again? Her gutsy mom set in motion a series of successes in Jennifer's life. She answered the calling to the stage in high school and continues to pursue a career in theater.

High Schoolers Learn a "Guts" Lesson

In chapter 2, I described the opening of our Leaders by Example training for high school students. Using different colored sunglasses, we help students understand the importance of how they view the world. I mentioned that we continue the day with exercises to help open their eyes to see the possibilities of who they can become.

Following the sunglass exercise, I ask three volunteers to come forward with no explanation of what I will ask of them. More times than not, one or two hands immediately shoot up, but it always seems harder to get the third student to come forward so I offer an encouragement: "I've found in the many years I've worked with your peers, the students who are quick to volunteer without knowing what I will ask of them are the students who go the farthest in life."

Hands start waving across the room.

Thrilled with their enthusiasm, I continue, "Here's another truth for you to hold on to. You will never know if you will succeed or fail at anything in life unless you're willing to try. If you think you might have an answer, offer it. Even if your answer is wrong, you get respect for trying. It takes gritty guts to be the first one to try anything."

For the rest of the day, many young adults who would normally remain silent speak up. The participation is over the top, acknowledged by teachers and administrators who note the level of engagement is heightened from the norm. We found this to be consistently true from one school group to the next. From public to private schools.

From time to time, I run into students who participated in Leaders by Example. Often, they point back to that opening day of training as life-changing. I hear comments like, "I found a new perspective on life," or "I've never forgotten the importance of having guts." I don't have room here to share all the stories of life application. Suffice it to say, the benefits of gritty guts are monumental.

Raising "Gritty" Kids with Guts

It doesn't take guts to be a parent, but it does take guts to parent. Your children need to see your gritty guts. When was the last time you stood up for the right against a wrong? Would your children say that you have guts? Have your children witnessed gutty behavior in you in combatting our culture? If you want your children to develop grit, it begins with your own willingness to be countercultural in your behavior, when culture is off-base.

As your children begin to see "gutsiness" in you, encourage the same in them. Beginning in the tyke years, encourage your child to extend his hand and say, "Nice to meet you," when introduced to someone new.

If your young child asks if she can have another slice of cake at a birthday party, encourage her to ask the hostess herself. On the way to school, remind your child to look for a classmate sitting alone and to be the one to offer to sit with them.

You can teach your elementary-age children the bully chant as a way to encourage them to stand up for a friend who is being bullied:

> Don't step back, step in, stand up. Don't let the bully beat him up.
> Fill his heart with all good stuff, then that bully won't be so tough.

Encouraging your children to use their guts to stand up is the foundation of grit. When your child knows you've got their back, they feel secure in who they are and whose they are. It is out of the security of your relationship that grit is developed.

R Is for RESILIENCE

The self-esteem movement has negatively affected the level of resilience in our children. Instead of building resilience in their hearts, parents try their best to keep kids from experiencing failure and disappointment. Consequently, we're raising WeakHearts—kids who crumble when they receive a lower-than-expected grade, lose a race, or must accept no as a final answer. Saddest of all, without the opportunity to work hard and overcome difficulties, today's children will never experience the joy of victory.

Technology has a role to play in the lack of resilience in our children. It seems mastering technology has become more important than learning basic skills in our youngest children. According to a study commissioned by internet security company AGV on how children aged two to five interact with technology, 69 percent can use a computer mouse, but only 11 percent can tie their own shoelaces. Fifty-eight percent know how to play a computer game, while only 52 percent can ride a bike and only 20 percent can swim. They found that our youngest boys and girls are equally adept at using technology.[5]

Without resilience, children are destined for lives of distress. A child who is lacking in resilience will be less comfortable taking risks. Children who are not resilient have difficulty controlling their emotions. Resilience is a stepping stone in the maturation process.

Let's properly define resilience and discuss what we can do to instill that can-do spirit in our children.

Helping Your Child Get Back Up

The *Oxford Dictionary* defines resilience as "the capacity to withstand or to recover quickly from difficulties; toughness."[6] This definition brings to mind the catchphrase for a favorite toy of the 1970s, "Weebles wobble, but they don't fall down."[7] Weebles—egg-shaped, roly-poly toys—were introduced in 1971 by Playskool. Skillfully designed with a weight located at the bottom-center that uprights the Weeble when it is tipped over, Weebles pop back up, no matter how hard the blow they receive.

Think of resilience as the weight in your son's soul that enables him to get back up when he's pushed down or the weight that enables your daughter to stand back up when her heart is broken.

Here's my best attempt at a working definition for us: resilience is the ability to bounce back from hardships, mistakes, defeat, and difficult experiences and grow from them. We want our children to not only bounce back, but to be positively shaped from overcoming difficulties.

Scripture tells us "that suffering produces perseverance; perseverance, character; and character, hope" (Rom. 5:3–4). With the explosion of mental health troubles in our young people, giving your children opportunities to grow resilience is critical to their well-being. Resilience brings hope, which is the ultimate protection for our children from becoming a sad statistic.

Good Risk-Taking

When we allow our children to run as fast as they can in circles, spin as hard as they can, roughhouse, and jump from heights that make us a bit nervous, we're helping them see themselves as capable and competent heroes in their own hearts.

We built a swing set in the backyard for our grandchildren a few years ago. On one side is a gym bar with handles that has gone unnoticed until recently. I should have known when our six-year-old granddaughter hollered, "GG, watch this . . ." I was going to be uncomfortable watching whatever she wanted to show me. When I looked over to see her little body hanging upside down, several feet off the ground, not looking old enough or strong enough for such a feat, my husband had to hold me back from rescuing her. (Of course, he was right.) She flipped off the bar, landed on her feet, and proclaimed, "I did it! I did it! I knew I could do it!"

When you're tempted to step in with another "be careful," try to resist the urge. Give your children the freedom to skin their knees, stub their toes, and land on their backside.

Trial and Error

From little things to big things. From tying shoes to doing homework to learning a new skill, allow your child to work at it without your help. Give them time and space to figure it out for themselves. When we jump in and do it for them, we're telling them we don't believe they're capable of doing it on their own.

Let your child get frustrated. I know it's hard to see them struggle, but we know as adults nothing worthwhile comes easy. Don't allow your child to give up because they have to work hard. Help them keep the end in mind. Remind them of how much they will enjoy being able to play the instrument or pass the test or how good it will feel to master something new. Remind them that everyone started somewhere.

Stories of trial and error are abundant: Thomas Edison, Abraham Lincoln, sports figures, early space travel, and your personal stories of struggling as a child to learn new skills.

One of my sons had a difficult teacher in fifth grade. Parents of two other students requested their children be moved to different classrooms. My son asked if he could move too. After much thought and prayer, I decided there was more to be gained by keeping him in this uncomfortable situation than moving him. His teacher was demanding, and at times unfair, but my son learned important life lessons during that year of adversity. When the year was over, he had the great satisfaction of knowing he earned the good grade he had been given.

Think back to watching your infant as he or she learned to walk and remember the process:

- Pulling up on every chair, sofa cushion, anything that helped to stay upright
- Moving along the edge of the chair or sofa to feel the ground under those little feet
- Letting go to see what would happen (the first thrill of risk-taking)
- Reaching for a hand to help walk across the room
- Taking those first steps without assistance

Think about what you did in this process. You watched. You cheered. You encouraged, but you did not, could not, take those first steps for your son or daughter. They had to do it on their own.

We serve our children well when we don't lose sight of the great benefit of trial and error in the learning process, especially as it relates to building the essential quality of resilience.

Problem-Solving

What do you do when your child gets in trouble? Maybe they got into an argument with a neighbor down the street or they made a mistake that needs restitution. Rather than jumping in with a solution, ask your child how the other person might be feeling about their actions. Then ask them to consider how best to solve the problem they have created. This is how we help our children grow from their mistakes.

When we help our children see failures as opportunities for learning, they discover they are not defined by their failures. They develop resilience in the face of disappointments and setbacks.

In an insightful article from Bright Horizons, we learn, "While children learn from mistakes, they also develop the self-confidence, self-concept, and moral judgement that comes from doing something like apologizing to the neighbor or working to right a wrong."[8]

Ask yourself what you are doing for your children that they could do themselves? Do you jump when they make a request they could handle on their own? When they're thirsty or lose something or drop something?

One of our granddaughters was at the kitchen island working on a project. The first time she dropped her marker and asked for my assistance, I stopped the work I was doing and retrieved it for her. The second time she dropped her marker and asked for my assistance, I said, "You'll have to get that one." She hesitated with a little bit of a huff, slid down from the barstool, and picked it up. It didn't happen again.

Not only did she learn to do for herself what she *could* do for herself, but she learned to pay attention to what she was doing!

We were leaving the community pool one afternoon with our daughter's family when our six-year-old grandson started complaining about being hungry with no reply from mom. He turned up the volume and his plea of being really hungry to being really, really hungry. Without slowing down, his mom turned and said, "Why don't you chew your elbow?"

I wish you could have seen him lifting his forearm to try and reach his elbow. He decided he could wait till later for a snack. He learned in that moment that he could find a way to deal with his distress. He found he had options in how to handle not getting what he wanted when he wanted it.

Children learn how to cope when they are given opportunities to experience disappointment. Without those opportunities, resilience is not built, leaving your children ill-equipped for the big disappointments and struggles that are part of growing up. When we make things too easy for our children, life becomes too hard.

I Is for INTEGRITY

Psychologist Henry Cloud offers an insightful definition of integrity in the title of his book *Integrity: Courage to Meet the Demands of Reality*.[9] I love this definition of integrity so much I'll repeat it: "Courage to meet the demands of reality." Integrity is owning your mistakes. It's listening to the opinions of others. It's a willingness to learn from others, to be teachable.

It seems to come as a pleasant surprise to a parent when they see integrity in their teenager. Not because they haven't given it all they've got in trying to instill integrity, but because they're not quite sure their teenager has been getting it, until they see it played out in his life. One mom shared such a moment:

> We are so thankful our son is a good kid. He's played sports since he was little, so we've always given his coaches credit for instilling a strong work ethic in him. He learned early in life to be your best; you

> have to give your best. Last week, he received an award at his workplace for his honesty and hard work. When I congratulated him, he floored me with this comment, "Mom, I wouldn't be the same person I am if you and Dad had given it all to me. Most of my friends don't get it because their parents haven't made them do anything. Not working teaches kids how not to work."

Be Who You Want Your Children to Become

Cloud directs our thinking with this insight, "To achieve is the child's responsibility, but to empower the child is the parent's responsibility. So, instead of just setting a standard, the parent of grace gives support, coaching, teaching, structure, modeling, help, and consequences to empower the child to get there."[10]

Children have a simple understanding of right and wrong. As concrete thinkers, they have a keen awareness of hypocrisy. The soul question for tweens in the "Home of Respect" chart, "Are you real?" is a critical component of instilling integrity in your child's heart. When our actions don't match our words, we impede the development of integrity. Saying "Do as I say, not as I do" is nonsense to our children because what we do drowns out what we say, every time.

Do you want your children to be the best they can be?
Expect nothing less of yourself.

Do you want your children to respect your word?
Keep your word.

Do you want your children to own their mistakes?
Own yours.

Do you want your children to be kind?
Be kind to everyone you meet.

Do you want your children to tell the truth?
Always tell the truth and live by truth.

Do you want your children to be unselfish?
Give generously of your time and effort.

Do you want your children to persevere?
Don't give up when the going gets tough.

Do you want your children to be patient?
Endure irritations with grace.

Do you want your children to respect others?
Be respectful of your spouse and children.

Do you want your children to work hard?
Work hard at all that you do.

We all make mistakes. None of us is perfect, in fact, far from it. But when our children see how we rectify our mistakes, how we live in truth, and how we accept instruction with the right attitude, they witness the working out of integrity.

You can be certain your integrity, more than your words, will be emulated by your children. Michele Borba, child psychologist, reminds us that "parents with clearly identified moral convictions are more likely to raise good kids. Because their kids know what their parents stand for and why they do, their kids are more likely to adopt their parents' beliefs. So begin by asking yourself what virtues and moral beliefs matter most to you."[11]

Hopefully, the virtue of hard work is on your list.

A Strong Work Ethic

Integrity begins with the development of a strong work ethic. If your children do chores, you're off to a great start.

I know a young adult who has a tremendous work ethic that came from the persuasive pressure of his grandpa. When he was seven years old, his grandpa offered him a portion of his vegetable garden with the promise that whatever he grew would be his to sell. Garett took him up on his offer. I'm pleased to say Garett helped with the cost of a pickup truck and half the price tag of a tractor in high school with money earned from planting, growing, shelling, and selling purple hull peas from his gardening endeavor. In addition to being a good student, he also found time to become a skilled jujitsu purple belt (as of this writing). He's now a college freshman majoring in engineering, selling purple hull peas, and teaching jujitsu classes as a way of sharing the sport he loves.

Garett didn't learn to plant and grow peas from reading a manual. He was given patient instruction and learned by watching his grandpa work his garden. To instill a strong work ethic takes time and patience on your part in the beginning; working alongside your child until they "get it." Then, letting them get after it on their own, knowing it will take time to get it right.

T Is for TENACITY

In defining tenacity as "the quality displayed by someone who just won't quit—who keeps trying until they reach their goal,"[12] I can describe my fifteen-year-old grandson as a tenacious young man.

Jack is becoming quite an accomplished swimmer. His mom passed her love of swimming on to her children. She is there at every meet punching a timer, manning the concessions, and cheering from the poolside.

Swimming as a competitive sport is new for me. I can tell you; I'm enthralled with it. Jack appreciates my interest and has done his best to help me understand the heat sheet. If you're not familiar with a swim meet heat sheet, each heat is listed with all swimmers' names and lanes. With several heats in each competition the sheet can look like row after row of names and numbers that are meaningless to a novice.

Fortunately, Jack took the time to explain the content of each column and the reason for the information, not just once, but several times in his first season. Now, just imagine, if sixty swimmers are competing in a day's meet, there will be ten events, each with six heats. The heat sheet for a swim meet is composed of several pages of information compiled into an ongoing document of names, events, lanes, and rankings. Confused yet? I was (and still can be at a state meet).

Events are broken down by distance (50, 100, 200, 500, 1,000, 1 mile), stroke (freestyle, backstroke, breaststroke, butterfly, or Individual Medley [IM]) and oftentimes by age, gender, and relay type.

After a recent event, Jack and I talked about his standing. The conversation went something like this:

"Jack, how did you do in the meet yesterday?"

Jack replied, "I came in first in the 100 Breaststroke."

With a pat on his back, I responded, "Way to go!"

"Yeah, but *even better*, I took six seconds off the 200 Breaststroke . . . six seconds. Not one, not two, not three, not four, not five, but *six* seconds!"

"So, you won that heat too?"

"No way. I was swimming against sixteen-year-olds. Didn't matter, 'cause I beat myself," he replied with a fist pump of satisfaction.

It felt good to beat his opponents, but it always feels better when he beats himself. Why? For Jack, happiness is winning a heat. Joy comes when he beats his personal best time in his favorite event, the breaststroke. For every heat that he shaves time, he comes a bit closer to his real goal—finding his personal best.

I asked Jack recently what it is about swimming that draws him to the sport. His answer: "I want to find out how good I can get. It's about how hard I'm willing to train." For Jack it's not competing against others that thrills him but competing against himself.

For anyone who might think swimming is an easy sport, consider Jack's new practice schedule: Monday through Friday from 4:30–6:45pm, along with Monday and Wednesday mornings from 5–6:30am. Saturday practice is dependent on the weekly practices. The swimming season is year-round, not a few months on and a few months off.

Jack has discovered the secret for finding joy—competing against himself, not others—to become the best that he can be, a true StrongHeart. I call this the principle of Personal Best.

The Quest for Personal Best

Just imagine the angst our children could avoid if we instilled the understanding Jack has—the only person you compete against is yourself.

It is nearly impossible in the image-obsessed world of social media our children are growing up in to not fall prey to comparison. What a safeguard you would give your child if you encouraged them to strive for their personal best. It wouldn't matter what anyone else is doing, what anyone else is getting or is given, or what anyone else is achieving.

The most beneficial aspect of striving for personal best is that it becomes a lifelong quest that propels your child to keep going because every day is an opportunity to learn something new, to be a bit kinder, to rectify yesterday's mistakes, or to be a little better than the day before.

Building Tenacity

Children need strategies and tactics to handle setbacks and to help themselves with challenging tasks or circumstances. Research suggests that teaching children to set a goal, plan the steps needed to accomplish the goal, and recognize that a course of action may be needed when setbacks occur, equips children to overcome setbacks and keep going. The following suggestions incorporate all the above strategies in the process of learning.

Memorization

An important life skill that has been lost is memorization. Only three decades ago, our minds were our database. I can't begin to count how many telephone numbers I held in my memory bank. I still know my home phone number from childhood. Calculators removed the need to do "math in your head." Computers drastically reduced, if not replaced, the learning tool of writing pencil to paper, which aided in the memorization of long passages.

What does memorization have to do with tenacity? First, the process of memorizing requires trial and error to accomplish the goal of moving new information from the short-term or working memory to long-term stored memory. Second, memorization enables a child to discover how much they can accomplish with a bit of effort. The "aha" moment when every word of the poem flows out of your child's mouth is more than a reason for a high five. Your child has just experienced the exhilaration of a job well done, knowing extra effort pays off.

Let me encourage you to begin at the age of four with Bible verses and nursery rhymes. My granddaughters have a memory box we made from a recipe box that holds their Bible verses. I write the verse on the top of an index card, leaving plenty of room for the girls to copy the verse once or twice below. After they have memorized the verse, we place it in their memory box. With each visit, they recite the previously learned verses and add another. Next step, the Ten Commandments and then, the Preamble to the Constitution.

Memorization accomplishes more than the storage of information. It is good for your child's brain development. Our brain is a pattern-seeking entity that encodes information, much the same way that an online search engine lifts words or phrases from your search history and then links you to related advertisements. Each time a connection is made, the path from one idea to the next is made clearer and the thought process improves. This is why practicing the piano makes a good pianist. The firing between the synapses speeds up and works better and better each time we use it.[13]

Creativity and Music

Craft projects are tenacity builders. Whether a simple building project or a more complex project like a model car or a dollhouse, cultivating a child's creative capacity encourages tenacity. Developing the mastery of any musical instrument takes time, effort, practice, and tenacity.

With short-term projects children learn that they *can* start and finish a project. With long-term projects, they learn the desired outcome won't happen if they quit.

Elizabeth Keller of Kids Discover says to "think of developing creativity like going to the gym and building your muscles; it doesn't happen overnight, but if you continually work those creativity muscles in your child's brain, they develop the propensity to think outside the box when faced with new problems to solve."[14]

Others Who Have Done It

Share with your children or students stories of children who grow up to do great things. For ages eight through twelve, the Lightkeepers[15] series offers inspiring stories of boys and girls who are just like them. Author Irene Howat tells of kids who find their purpose and pursue it with their whole hearts.

Using real-life stories encourages your children to not give up on their dreams. When my sons were in middle school, the phrase "everybody started somewhere" became the encouragement in times of disappointment. They would be reminded that Babe Ruth broke the record of most home runs (60) and struck out more than any other player (89) in the same season—the point being, he gave it all he had every time he stepped up to the plate.

We talked about the lives of Eric Liddell, Albert Einstein, Abraham Lincoln, George Washington Carver, Walt Disney, Sir John Oldcastle, and many sports heroes. Each one gave a different perspective on what it takes to become all you are meant to be. It is in the striving for personal best that your children can find God's purpose for their lives. Rather than ask your child what they would like to be when they grow up, ask them who they believe God created them to be based on their interests, gifts, and talents.

Rather than ask your child what they would like to be when they grow up, ask them who they believe God created them to be based on their interests, gifts, and talents.

In a moment of inspiration, one of my grandchildren made the remark, "God made me to be an artist and a scientist."

"How do you know?" I asked.

"Because I love to do art and I like to figure things out. I don't know why I like those things, but I do, so God must have put them in my heart," she replied with a nod of certainty.

Learning to Fail

Protecting our children from failure does more harm than good. The inability to handle failure prevents your child from learning coping skills for the larger disappointments that will come in the teen years. You can help your child understand that failing brings them one step closer to learning valuable lessons from their mistakes.

You've probably heard Thomas Edison's famous quote about the lightbulb, but it won't hurt to be reminded. The story is told that in the 1920s, a journalist asked Thomas Edison how it felt to fail a thousand times in his attempt to invent the incandescent lightbulb. He replied, "I didn't fail 1,000 times. The lightbulb was an invention with 1,000 steps."[16]

Here's two more quotes from Thomas Edison, you can use with your children:

> "Negative results are just what I want. They're just as valuable to me as positive results. I can never find the thing that does the job best until I find the ones that don't."[17]
>
> "Many of life's failures are people who did not realize how close they were to success when they gave up."[18]

Follow these guidelines in helping your child fail forward toward success:

- Don't criticize your child for failing. Empathize with their disappointment.
- Share stories of your failures in life and how you handled setbacks.
- Remind your child that a failure is just a detour sign, not a stop sign.
- Remind your child that failing teaches us lessons that make life better.
- Failing helps us grow stronger.
- When you laugh at yourself, others laugh with you, not at you.
- No one is good at everything. We can each be good at something.

Encourage your child to develop a creative solution to the problem at hand. Beyond life lessons learned, competence that is gained in overcoming failure remains into adulthood.

GRIT Is So Much More

It's GUTS that enables your child to try something new, to offer someone their help, or even to answer a question in class.

It's RESILIENCY that gives your child the ability to bounce back from hardships, defeat, and difficult experiences and grow from them.

It's INTEGRITY that encourages your child to own their mistakes, to listen and learn from the opinions of others, and to maintain a teachable heart.

And, it's TENACITY that keeps your child from quitting when others quit to find joy in fulfilling God's purpose for their life.

If your deepest desire is to raise a StrongHeart who can overcome the distractions, the disappointments, and the disservice of our culture to become all they are meant to be, you must help your child develop GRIT—Guts. Resiliency. Integrity. Tenacity.

CHAPTER EIGHT

Practice Others-Centeredness

STRONG, adj. *Having great force of mind, of intellect or of any faculty; as a man of strong powers of mind; a man of a strong mind or intellect; a man of strong memory, judgment, or imagination.*[1]

We live in a cul-de-sac with one neighbor to our right and three neighbors to our left. We found a ziplock bag in our mailbox recently containing a note, a dollar bill, and several coins, totaling $2.02. Written across the top of the note was "MOM." There wasn't a sentiment on the note, only the signature "Walt" in a child's handwriting. It appeared that our five-year-old neighbor, Walt, had signed the note, so my husband walked over to return the bag to its rightful owner, or so we thought.

As it turned out, Walt's keen ears and tender heart had been in tune to the chatter around him about elevated costs at the grocery, outrageous bills at the pharmacy, and soaring prices at the gas pump. Having recently celebrated a birthday, he wanted to share his birthday money with his neighbors to help us pay for gas. Even though they were already late for school, Walt's dad was pleased to assist his son in spreading a little joy.

A precious others-centered heart resides in this perceptive child. He saw a need, recognized he could help, and offered his help. He wasn't looking for recognition, a thank you, or anything in return. No matter what the years ahead hold for Walt, I doubt he will ever forget the day he helped us all. We will certainly never forget.

Walt has experienced the truth of Dr. Henry Cloud's statement, "The end of oneself, the end of self-interest, is the beginning of an even greater self"[2] at the tender age of five.

Here's a story from *Reader's Digest* of another others-centered young man told by the gentleman who experienced his kindness:

> Leaving a store, I returned to my car only to find that I'd locked my keys and cell phone inside. A teenager riding his bike saw me kick a tire and say a few choice words. "What's wrong?" he asked. I explained my situation. "But even if I could call my wife," I said, "she can't bring me her car key, since this is our only car." He handed me his cell phone.
>
> "Call your wife and tell her I'm coming to get her key."
>
> "That's seven miles round trip."
>
> "Don't worry about it."
>
> An hour later, he returned with my key. I offered him some money, but he refused.
>
> "Let's just say I needed the exercise," he said. Then, like a cowboy in the movies, he rode off into the sunset.[3]

This selfless teenager no doubt had the same perspective Walt has on life.

Allow one more story about a young girl who was in tune with a friend's hurt feelings.

Second graders had just presented a sweet song at their school's Friday morning chapel service. Parents and guests were invited to gather in the courtyard before the children returned to their classes. One of the little girls burst into tears when her parents had to leave for work. One of her parents' friends tried to console her to no avail.

A classmate rushed over and put her arm around her friend, and said, "Don't cry, hug these little guys. They'll make you feel better," as she passed on her two favored stuffed animals, she had brought to school for story time that day. Her little friend nodded her head and said, "Okay, if you say so." The kind little girl kept her arm around her classmate as they walked to their room. By the time they arrived, the tears were gone. When the little girl tried to return the stuffed animals to their rightful owner, the generous classmate said, "They can keep you company till story time."

What quality do each of these admirable young people have in common? Empathy: the foundation of an others-centered perspective on life.

Empathy Feels the Pains and Joys of Others

Merriam-Webster defines empathy as, "the action of understanding, being aware of, being sensitive to, and vicariously experiencing the feelings, thoughts, and experiences of another."[4] In other words, an empathetic person feels the pains *and* the joys of others. When our little second grader felt the pain of her classmate's aching heart, she gave love and support from the depths of her heart.

How can you help your child develop empathy? Studies have shown the development of empathy begins by the age of two. Another important aspect of chores, as discussed in chapter 5, is that chores are a way of helping children break through their self-centered worldview. Beginning with the simple request of your two-year-old to hang up their towel each day so the next person doesn't have to clean up after them helps children to see how their actions affect others. Learning to help others begins with honoring a request to help someone else. As a child enters pre-K, their world begins expanding. The satisfaction gained from learning to help others becomes the motivation to reach out and help without being asked to help. When they see a classmate in need of assistance, they offer to help.

"Children aren't born with empathy, and it can take time to develop. In the meantime, they may view themselves as the center of the universe," pediatrician Jonathan Williams says, "as evidenced by the terrible twos and 'threenager' phases. Most toddlers aren't leaping to clean up their toys."[5]

When your children are unkind to each other, grab their attention and ask, "How would you feel if your brother called you such an ugly name?" or "How do you think your sister felt when you grabbed her doll without asking?" Wait for their answers, then encourage them to think for a few minutes about how they would feel if the shoe was on the other foot.

With children five and older, I recommend doing the StrongHeart lesson with them, as I did with my youngest granddaughters. When your children "see" the heart filled with "bad stuff" you can explain that whenever they see a friend, classmate, or neighbor acting unkindly or feeling sad, they can remember that trouble on the outside means there's a struggle on the inside. Rather than being offended by the actions of the one in distress, encourage your child to ask the other person if they're okay or if they need help.

As your children move toward the tween years, look for ways they can get outside themselves to see the unspoken needs of others. My sons learned how to see with the eyes of their hearts one scorching hot August day in Louisiana.

When my twin sons were ten years old, we dropped off clothes at the cleaners near our home. The ladies who served us were dripping in sweat. You could see the steam seeping through the doors behind the counter. When I commented how extremely hot it was in the store, one of the ladies shared that the air conditioner had gone out and could not be repaired until the next day.

When we got in the car, one of my sons said, "Mom, I wish there was something we could do for those ladies. They looked miserable."

"You know what. There *is* something we can do," I answered. "Let's grab an ice chest from the house and—" Before I could finish, the boys jumped in to say, "We can fill it up with ice and water bottles."

"Can we give them snacks too? I know they must be hungry from working in the heat!" added the other son.

Within a half hour, we were back at the cleaners. I stayed in the car, while the boys carried in the ice chest, along with a sack of treats. Watching from the distance, I couldn't tell who had the bigger smiles, the ladies or my sons. From where I was sitting, it looked like they were all celebrating the joy that empathy brings. The ladies were grateful beyond words, and the boys never forgot how good they felt when they returned to the car.

Looking with the eyes of their hearts became a lifelong holy habit in both. Empathy enables your child to not only sense the suffering of others, but also their triumphs.

Empathy Shares the Joys of Others

An empathetic child also rejoices with those who rejoice. Celebrating the joys of others is the flipside of empathy. Encourage your children to congratulate their classmate that receives an award or recognition. Remind your children to congratulate the members of the other team for winning rather than worrying about their team's loss. Urge your children to cheer others on in competitive situations.

Olympic gold medalist Eric Liddell, memorialized in *Chariots of Fire*, was widely known for his gentlemanly ways, his unwavering faith, and his record-setting speed on the track. Before each race, his humble confidence was evident as he shook hands with each of his competitors and introduced himself, wishing them well. It was natural for him, but in the world of competitive sports it was completely unexpected.

Teach your children at any age the "Words of Wonder" to share with a sibling, classmate, or team member. We call it giving a WOW! Help your children learn the following phrases:

- WOW, way to go!
- WOW, you were awesome!
- WOW, good job!
- WOW, nice going!
- WOW, good game!

Your child can add three rapid-fire high fives to their words of celebration to underscore their excitement.

Teaching your children to recognize how others are feeling and to reach out with words of encouragement or celebration takes the focus off themselves. Rather than worrying about how others are treating them, they find greater satisfaction in living by the "Golden Rule" of treating others the way they want to be treated.

Instilling Empathy

Looking for a few do-it-right-now tips. Look no further:

Tykes: three to five

- Work on social skills. The common courtesies of respect: "Yes, sir," "Yes, ma'am," "Thank you," "Please," "Excuse me."

- When there's a fuss between siblings, ask them to swap shoes, and literally walk in the other person's shoes. (I know the size difference, but no matter, they can at least attempt to put their foot in the other sibling's shoe!) Remind them of the Golden Rule: treat their sibling the way they themselves want to be treated. To look at the situation from their sibling's point of view. Amazing how even young children can gain a different perspective from this exercise.
- You've heard it before, but assigning chores that benefit the entire family, not just your child picking up after himself, opens your child's heart to others. Feeding the family pet. Bringing in the newspaper or mail. Putting away groceries.

Pre-tweens: six to ten

- Help your child make a collage of different facial expressions and identify the emotions behind each face. Talk about how to respond to someone who is sad, angry, excited, etc.
- Check our reading list for recommendations of books that show your child what empathy looks like, such as the classic, *Charlotte's Web* by E. B. White.
- Model empathy in your interactions with others.

Tweens: eleven to thirteen

- Give more responsibility.
- Hold family meetings that allow each member of the family to take a turn sharing what's going on in their hearts. Celebrate the wins and offer encouragement in the struggles.
- Express an interest in your children's friends and families. Use a calendar to keep up with important happenings, so you can inquire about the outcomes.

Teens: thirteen+

- Encourage your teen to jump in and help in small ways and big ways, as our thoughtful teen did when he helped the man who locked his keys and phone in his car.
- Volunteer with your teen in your community.
- Set aside one day a month for the whole family to volunteer together. We have a group that does an afternoon walk to deliver meals from the back of a long-bed truck in our poorest neighborhoods. All ages participate. Children shoot baskets. Men throw footballs.

The only purpose is to connect through love.

The process of helping your children move from their innate self-centeredness to others-centeredness brings us to the most important of all parenting questions: Which will you choose, to raise your children in the mirror or through the window?

We took a glimpse at this question in chapter 2. A fuller understanding is critical in your quest to raise a StrongHeart.

Which Will You Choose, the Mirror or the Window?

Let's first turn our attention to the mirror and the results of raising your child behind its silver lining. Much has been written about looking in the mirror to see our faults and find answers to life. But the truth is . . . no answers are found in a mirror, only more questions.

Jordan Scott, assistant editor of *USGlass* magazine writes, "In ancient times, mirrors were made from expensive metals. Now, mirrors are most often made by covering flat glass with a reflective coating, such as silver. Glass provides a solid base for mirrors due to its smooth surface and rigidity. Plus, it's relatively easy to make. The glass used must be polished, and without imperfections."[6]

To understand how ordinary glass becomes a mirror, Scott explains, "The first step in the process is cutting the glass to shape and size, which can vary greatly depending on application. Once the glass is the correct shape, size and smoothness, the reflective coating is applied in an evaporator, or large vacuum chamber. The metal is heated to the point that it evaporates, depositing a coating onto the glass surface."[7]

The glass that once offered a view clear through will now be used to show only a reflection of the viewer. Just as the wicked queen in the story of Snow White found a mirror magnified her self-obsession, so the mirror of self-esteem magnifies your child's innate self-absorption.

As we discussed earlier, when we seek to build our child's self-esteem, we place a mirror in their hands and say, "Take a look, it's all about you. What you feel and what you want." But we know the longer one gazes in a mirror, the worse things look, don't we? The longer your child lives in the mirror, the more lost they become in themselves, becoming either self-conceited or self-conscious.

Lost in Self-Conceit

When we were in school, we all knew the person who thought too highly of himself, didn't we? The ball hog. The girl chaser. The girl who was stuck on herself. The leader of the mean girls. The gossip. The kid who wanted the rest of us to bow at their feet in awe and reverence.

Today, this kid doesn't just make remarks behind a classmate's back or pull innocent enough pranks (which were still harmful). Today, this kid goes after the one being teased to destroy them emotionally. The sense of entitlement is exacerbated with the loss of respect for others and the lack of respect for self. Kids who have no moral compass with which to restrain their behavior are easily persuaded to participate in illicit activities.

Mirror children who become self-conceited expect parents and others to cater to their every whim. They are demanding, strong-willed children who are hypersensitive to any form of discomfort or criticism. Sadly, with each act of selfishness, their hearts are not filled, but emptied.

Lost in Self-Consciousness

Mirror children who have become self-conscious are fixated on their flaws. They can't see who they are meant to be and can't find the unique abilities they've been given to add value to the world. They fall into destructive behavior patterns that destroy them mentally, physically, emotionally, and spiritually. From drugs to sexual encounters, from cutting to tech addiction.

Operating out of fear of missing out, fear of being overlooked, or fear of not fitting in, their lives become filled with more questions than answers.

Children who become lost in themselves are unable to distinguish their feelings from reality. When pressed deeper into their thoughts, they perceive their feelings to be truth and reality to be a lie. The world is asking your children what they are feeling and encouraging them to act on their feelings. To counter, you must acknowledge their feelings but help them find the truth upon which they can stand. Timeless, absolute truth has always been true and always will be. Truth doesn't change as culture changes or generations proceed.

The truth is, feelings and truth are often in opposition to each other. Feelings come and go due to circumstances or shifting societal mores. Truth is the insulation your child needs to keep from falling prey to the lies of those around them who do not have their best interest in mind.

Your child may feel hopeless, but the truth is, there is hope beyond their misery. There is a tomorrow beyond today. There is truth to combat the lies of their feelings.

Lost in Themselves

A report from Cigna found that young adults are much more likely to experience loneliness than the generations before them. A staggering 79 percent of Gen Zers (born 1997–2010) reported feeling lonely, compared to 71 percent of Millennials (born 1981–1996) and 50 percent of Boomers (born 1946–1964).[8] The esteeming of ourselves has certainly contributed to these statistics, not to mention how it has greatly affected our ability to esteem others. To connect. To love. To give. To live.

The truth is . . . we were not wired to esteem ourselves.

Behind the mirror our children can't see others or the needs of others, and they can't see others looking at them. This is the explanation of the loneliness and isolation that is plaguing our teenagers and young adults today.

Mirror kids are screaming at the rest of us through their extreme behavior, begging us to see who they really are—lost kids in need of truth. Kids who desperately want to understand right from wrong. They are looking for absolute truth on which to build their lives. They want to know what is right and wrong.

So, what if we put the mirrors down? What if we help our children see beyond themselves? What if we lead our children to the window?

The Window of Self-Respect

In *Raising Unselfish Children in a Self-Absorbed World*, I share a synopsis of *The Secret Garden* that gives us a glimpse into what happens when children begin to view life through a window. They see their own reflection in the glass, but immediately see beyond themselves to find themselves. Allow me to share it now with you.

> Mary Lennox was a most disagreeable child. A classic "aristobrat." And rightly so. Her father was a high-ranking British government official in India. Her self-indulgent mother found little time for her

daughter because she was always busy with social functions, beauty treatments, and gazing in her mirror.

Mary never smiled. She raised herself while servants looked after her needs. She could have anything she desired, with one exception, the attention of her parents. By the time she was ten she was filled with arrogant bitterness, so self-consumed she demanded that others bow to her every whim.

Mary's aunt and uncle, Archibald and Lilias Craven, lived on a beautiful country estate in Yorkshire, England, with their son, Colin. Lilias was a wonderful mother. She lived her days sharing the wonder of God's creation with her husband and son in their garden. Tragically, Lilias passed away when Colin was a young child. In deep grief, Archibald withdrew into himself, closing his heart to Colin and the gate of the garden to all.

When a cholera epidemic in India took the lives of Mary's parents, she was sent to live with her Uncle Archibald. There she found her cousin to be as miserable as she was. Ten-year-old Colin had not walked since his mother died. He spent his days in bed, convinced he would contract a terrible disease, self-absorbed in his fear. His father spent his days traveling through Europe to escape his pain. Colin longed for his father's affection. Instead, servants waited on him hand and foot, literally, in order to keep him calm and satisfied.

One foggy morning Mary discovered the gate and entered the garden. She walked among the overgrown weeds and forgotten plants. Her heart beat a new rhythm at the thought of bringing the garden back to life for Colin and his father. She longed to give herself in service, so that she might forget her own misery.

With the help of a new friend, Dickon, Mary spent her days pulling weeds and planting new flowers. She poured herself into the garden, finding a new life through giving rather than taking.

Mary shared her newfound exuberance for life with Colin, urging him to look out the window of his bedroom and to venture into the world beyond. She encouraged him to "get over himself" and come help in the garden, as a gift for his father and to honor his mother's memory. Mary's love for the garden gave Colin the courage to try.

With Mary and Dickon's encouragement, Colin made daily trips to the garden in his wheelchair. No longer did his window serve as a reminder of the world that had left him behind, it was a passageway to freedom as light poured in each morning bringing new opportunities.

As days passed, the children's former self-centeredness turned to self-forgetfulness. Achy muscles and hot temperatures didn't deter their work. The misery that had consumed their minds disappeared as their hearts filled with compassion. They stopped dwelling on what they didn't have, because they found what they needed, a purpose beyond themselves in serving others.

Colin soon found the courage to put his feet on the ground. His legs quivered under the weight of his body as he took his first steps. Just like a newborn lamb who finds his legs, Colin's wobble soon became a steady gait.

Receiving word that his son desperately needed him, Archibald rushed back to the estate to find Colin running to meet him. His son's unselfish love broke through Archibald's self-inflicted prison and set him free.[9]

Frances Hodgson Burnett's timeless characters in *The Secret Garden* lost their self-centeredness and became who they were meant to be when they looked beyond themselves to discover their purpose. As Mary worked tirelessly to restore the garden to its former beauty, she found God's purpose for her life in His creation. Archibald's heart opened to see how much his son needed him to be a real father. And Colin? He found the courage to become who he was created to be when he "got over himself" and bravely left his sorrows behind for joy in the newfound world beyond his window.

When your children look through a window at the world beyond, as Colin did, their own image will be reflected back to them in the glass, but in the appropriate context, as part of the world, not the center of the world. What's behind them quickly dissipates. Their present circumstance becomes a reflection of their future, rather than a reminder of their past.

Window children feel an obligation to others and a responsibility to society. They find joy in esteeming others and choose to give respect in all interactions. With each offering of respect, their self-respect deepens. Window children choose respect,

- regardless of the actions of the other person,
- even in the face of disrespect,
- in the home, at school, and in the community.

Bullies can't rock their foundation because kids who have self-respect know who they are and what they stand for. An others-centered viewpoint yields a stable view of the world and their place in it. They experience the joy of "doing nothing from rivalry or conceit, but in humility count others more significant than themselves. They look not only to their own interests, but also to the interests of others."[10] Satisfaction doesn't come from what they get but from what they give. Confidence is balanced with humility, evidenced in humble confidence.

Window children can see God and they can see God looking at them, which leads them to discover His purpose for their lives. They recognize an absolute truth from which to build their lives, which gives a moral compass that guides their decisions.

Hopelessness is replaced with hope.

Regardless of the individual purpose for each of our children, they become eager to step into the world beyond the window to love others as they have been loved.

Who Was I Created to Be?

When my sons were youngsters, we hosted a twist on a Halloween costume party. We opted for something a bit less scary than ghosts and goblins, but still a lot of fun. The invitations asked, "Who will you be when you grow up?" and invited kids to look far beyond themselves.

The kids came dressed as nurses, a college professor, an actress, a ballerina, a doctor, a dad, a fireman, an astronaut, and a few others. We played charades with the kids acting out each other's chosen profession. It was highly entertaining to watch five-year-olds depict grown-ups in their professional roles.

Who will you be when you grow up is a question that I believe we are born with deep in our souls. It's the first and the last soul question.

Remember the soul questions our children are looking to us to answer?

- Can I trust you?
- Who's in charge?
- Are you watching me?
- Who do I belong to?
- Do you really love me?
- Are you real?
- Who am I?
- Can I be in charge?

As our children grow, if we are intentional, we can satisfy the answers to these questions. But the question of who your child will become is beyond our scope of understanding. It's the big one. It's the question underneath all the rest. This is the one that all others emanate from. You and I don't have the answer to this one.

Perhaps a better way of asking this question is "Who was I created to be?" Isn't that the real question we all wonder about? Two of my granddaughters brought this to my attention one day.

Holding paintbrushes and making sweeping motions reminiscent of the great masters, they were having a grand time in the backyard painting rainbows, flowers, trees, and grass on either side of a children's easel.

The request to paint had followed the modeling clay bakery that served "real" pastries, which had followed the restaurant with its "world famous soup," which came after . . . you get the idea. Their imaginations were operating in hyper-mode.

As the girls continued to paint, one of them suddenly shouted, "GG, did you know God made me to be an artist?"

"Oh, He did, did He?" I replied with an agreeable chuckle. "How do you know?"

She scrunched her face, tilted her head, and replied, "I'm not sure, but I think it's because I like to paint."

While I was trying to formulate a wise response, her sister chimed in, "God made me to be an artist *and* a scientist."

"Oh, really now," I responded, "And how do you know?"

"Well, God made me, so He must need me to do something for Him."

Funny how children know what they know, isn't it?

Why not forgo the "What do you want to be when you grow up?" question and replace it with "Who were you created to be?" with your children. What a grand way to lead your children on a lifelong pursuit to find their identity and "do something for Him." You'll be well equipped to lead them when you choose the window of God's grace as the place to raise your children. It's through His window where they'll find who they are *meant* to be.

Reframing Your Children's Viewpoint

It is up to us to make sure we help our children put the mirror of self-destruction down and live through the window of God's grace. Take a look at the comparison of the two viewpoints:

In the Mirror	**Through the Window**
I only see me	I see others
No one sees the real me	Others can see me
I only see my needs	I see the needs of others
I become lost in myself	I see beyond myself
I'm hopeless	I'm hopeful
I see only impossibilities	I see the possibilities
I ask what the world is going to do for me	I ask what I can do for the world
Today is a reflection of the past	Today is a reflection of my future
I'm self-centered	I'm others-centered
I ask, "Who am I?"	I find out who I am!

Others-centered children see the possibilities of who they can become, knowing their worth is not found in what the world gives them, but in what they contribute to the world. Their satisfaction and fulfillment in life will come from finding God's purpose for their lives so that they can help others find His purpose for their lives.

CHAPTER NINE

Champion Respect

STRONG, adj. *Able; furnished with abilities.*[1]

The week I was planning to turn in this manuscript, I was captivated by a message delivered in a Sunday morning service by Gerrit Scott Dawson. His stinging words of truth touched every person of every generation. He delivered a powerful punch to parents and grandparents, young professionals and retirees, marrieds and singles. He zeroed in on one of the great struggles in raising children today: how to stop the frenetic activity in children that leads to fragility in teens and young adults.

In preparing the message, he asked clinical therapist Nathan Maranto his thoughts on the mental health of teens and young adults in our out-of-control culture. As an experienced social worker licensed to diagnose and treat mental, behavioral, and emotional disorders, Maranto explained that many adolescents "do not know their own strength, grit, or resiliency. They know their triggers but seem to buckle in front of them. . . . Young people see life as happening to them, not them happening to life."[2]

This astute therapist gave a graphic illustration of the kids he is seeing in his practice, "Often, I feel like I am trying to help lambs find wolf teeth."[3]

Captivated by his metaphor, I called to ask a few questions. In our conversation, he shared that many of the young people he works with are easily swayed by whatever is presented to them. They give Dissociative Identity Disorder (DID) promoted by TikTok as the answer to their confusion. When pressed to explain how they've come to that conclusion, they can't give an explanation for their feelings. They just "know" what they're feeling but have no basis for their feelings.

I asked how he reaches them. His short answer is to help them see the fallacy in their thinking by uncovering the truth.

My heart breaks, as I'm sure yours does too, that today's young people are growing up in a culture of lies. They're being pressed from all sides that whatever they are feeling is the truth. As adults, we know that is rarely true!

Without a belief system that informs their thinking, all they have are their feelings. That bears repeating: *without a belief system that informs their thinking, all they have are their feelings.* Unless their hearts are filled with truth from which they can form their opinions on life, they're helpless lambs who fall prey to predators. Lambs who can be manipulated to follow the crowd wherever the crowd is going because they have no path of their own to follow.

What an accurate word picture of WeakHearts who desperately want/need to be shepherded—WeakHearts yearning to develop "wolf teeth" so they can bite back and not be devoured by our culture.

This has been the purpose of this book—to equip you to help protect and prepare your children so that they can defend their beliefs and defeat their foes as StrongHearts who affect the world for good without becoming infected by it.

In this closing chapter we will highlight families who take their duty to their children seriously with firmness, fairness, and fun, along with a few other truths.

Leaders by Example

Dale and Lindy Weiner raised three children to adulthood, each of whom are enjoying married life with children of their own. The Weiners are a close family with a legacy of integrity, hard work, and generosity. A third generation is now following in the footsteps of their parents and grandparents.

I asked for an interview to find out how they did it.

One of the first questions I posed to this admirable couple was, "Which of the following was the most important heart attribute in raising your family—humility, respect, or resiliency—and why?" It brought different but harmonious answers. In unison, they responded, "Respect" (Lindy), "Resiliency" (Dale).[4]

"Respect. Without a doubt, respect," Lindy said. "Respect was an unspoken rule that our children understood without a lot of explanation. And it seems to me that respect is the foundation of resiliency, and for certain, humility."

Dale chimed in, "Resiliency. I wanted our children to be resilient. I wanted them to know how to accept bad outcomes by learning to fail."

Dale, a praiseworthy high school football coach, surpassed three hundred wins in his illustrious career, including multiple state and regional titles. It was not a surprise that resiliency would resonate in his heart. He felt the same duty to his players that he felt to his own children, an opportunity to mold them into resilient adults who could overcome the trials of life.

"Our children never wanted to disappoint their dad," Lindy interjected. "They had great respect for him because he respected the rules. As a high school coach, it was important to him to never do anything that would cause embarrassment to his family or to his school."

"I guess that's true," Dale reluctantly agreed. "I wanted our kids to understand what not to do, with the emphasis if you do wrong things or break rules, you won't have success in life." With a pause of deep thought, he added, "I do believe parents must model 'right' behavior."

Dale continued, "When children see the right way to do things, they easily recognize the ways that are wrong and those that will not serve them well. When they are taught the truths, they will not be easily fooled."

Even with the rigorous schedule of a coach, he found a way to be at the dinner table most nights and home on Saturdays. His success on the football field was unmatched by his success in leading his family to victory. The Weiners' son, Neil, now a high school coach in his own right, is leading his team to victory with the same integrity and leadership he learned from his father.

No doubt, the Weiners built their home on a foundation of mutual, abiding respect. And, no doubt, both Dale and Lindy modeled lives of humility and resiliency for their children to emulate.

One of Dale's comments stood out to me: "When children see the right way to do things, they easily recognize the ways that are wrong and those that will not serve them well." Let me offer a sad but true case study to prove Dale's point.

Parents Who Failed to Lead

Thirteen-year-old Ashley's (fictitious name) parents were gravely concerned. She had been gravitating to a new set of friends. She said her old friends were boring. Ashley's attitude toward her family was changing too. She started spending more time in her bedroom than in the living room. Her schoolwork was suffering.

Her parents were mystified. They had been "good" parents who spent a lot of time with their son and daughter through their growing up years. They sacrificed to send their children to a private school. Ashley had participated in dance, soccer, tennis, and a few other sports along the way. They had always been a family that spent time together. Even with busy work and social schedules, they included their children in many of their social activities.

After several sessions with a qualified counselor and hours of deep soul searching, Ashley's parents faced a hard reality: 90 percent of their parenting time had been spent entertaining their children, while only 10 percent had been spent training them in truth. These well-meaning parents didn't have Dale's conviction to teach "the right way to do things," so their daughter could "easily recognize the ways that were wrong and would not serve her well."

With all the best intentions, Ashley's parents had not made training a priority. They didn't have family devotions or long conversations around the dinner table. They didn't make time for teaching opportunities. Ashley grew up without solid direction and without an understanding of the values of her parents. They allowed the fun and excitement of busyness to fill their daughter's heart with the messages of the world.

When the preteen years hit, Ashley wasn't equipped to stand against ideas presented by her friends that didn't "feel" right. She was easily persuaded by others who were more adept at promoting lies than she was at defending truth. Ashley questioned her identity. An understanding of absolute rights and absolute wrongs was missed in her upbringing. Consequently, she could not discern truth from lie.

Amidst all the busyness, Ashley's parents hadn't taken the time to be intentional and purposeful in their parenting. Unlike another family who is finding a way with the help of a committed grandma.

The Power of a Grandparent's Influence

Grandparents can be just as much a part of parenting with intention as parents. The example of this grandma's intention can be emulated by parents.

A dear friend watched her grandson for the first three years of his life to help with childcare, until her own cancer diagnosis put that on hold. Now, six years later, this generous grandmother picks him up from school almost every day. She has taught him to have a quiet time for reading the Bible, prayer, and journaling his thoughts before he dives into homework. This thoughtful young man put the Scriptures he learns in his ball bag.

At the age of nine, her grandson is a gifted athlete. He struggles a bit with the urge to show off his talents and shake off his mistakes. His grandma has talked to him at length about his attitude. She has taught him to ask God to help him do his best and to show self-control and exhibit leadership.

In a recent baseball game, he was having a stellar performance with a three-inning no-hitter. Between the third and fourth innings, fatigue was setting in, so as he sat in the dugout he bowed his head in prayer. During the top of the fourth inning, his coach (who is also his dad) recognized his struggle and called a time-out. The catcher, first baseman, and shortstop joined him on the mound with his son who asked if they could pray together. This budding StrongHeart led them in prayer.

Parents Are Still the Greatest Influence

With every family I interviewed, and those I have closely observed, the greatest influence on a child's development is still the parents.

Dads who are not present (whether home or not) leave a scar on their children's hearts. Moms who are abrasive build resentment in their children's hearts. Parents who dole out empty threats leave children confused about how they are expected to behave.

Dads who lead their family with integrity instill respect in their children's hearts. Moms who are kindhearted instill kindness in their children's hearts. Parents who are consistent in their discipline instill self-discipline in their children.

Today's children benefit from good parenting or suffer from poor parenting, just as we did. Character-centered and Developer parents are two models of good parenting. In my book *Raising Respectful Children in a Disrespectful World,* I give definitions of each:

> Character-centered parents are more concerned with their child's character than their comfort. They understand that "children come into the world needing guidance to become all they were created to be. They need direction. They need examples to follow. Children need someone to nurture their souls and protect their hearts. They need someone who will offer real answers. They need someone to walk beside them every step of the way with encouragement. Children need more than the world has to offer."[5]

Developer parents take charge of their role as parents and parent. They understand that only being a friend to their children will be detrimental to their development. They take their role as teacher seriously, and make decisions for their children until their children are mature enough to make decisions for themselves.[6]

The blending of the Developer parents and Character-centered parents as teachers and guides gives us a full picture of effective parenting. The ability to apply persuasive pressure that protects and prepares your child is the secret ingredient in character-centered parenting that develops a StrongHeart.

Persuasive Pressure

We know that diamonds are the hardest of gemstones. Rubies are a close second. Unlike diamonds, rubies are one of the rarest of gemstones and are formed from extreme heat and excessive pressure in the depths of the earth. "When compressed, oxygen and aluminum atoms turn into corundum. This mineral, along with the presence of chromium, creates rubies and their distinctive hue."[7]

Geology Science gives us a foundational understanding of the fascinating background of rubies:

> Essentially, the correct ingredient combination, pressure, and heat must last long enough for rubies to form. In addition to heat and pressure, rubies need room to grow. In ancient times, rubies were used in royal and religious objects. The ancient Greeks believed wearing a ruby would help preserve mental health and protect its wearer from harm. During the Middle Ages, ruby was considered to have healing powers and was often used to treat various ailments.[8]

The name *ruby* comes from the Latin word *ruber*, which means "red." In an article "Ruby History and Lore" from the Gemological Institute of America, we find that "the glowing red of ruby suggested an inextinguishable flame burning in the stone. . . . Early cultures believed rubies held the power of life because of their similarity to blood, and rubies are mentioned four times in the Bible, associated with attributes like beauty and wisdom."[9]

It seems most fitting to use the formation of a ruby gemstone as a metaphor for the formation of a StrongHeart. Just as heat and pressure are needed to uncover a stone of great value, persuasive pressure is needed to raise a child to become a StrongHeart, a morally courageous young person, grounded in truth, who can withstand the temptations of the world to become all God created them to be.

"Persuasion" in the original Greek meant to stir belief in others through words. Proverbs 16:23 tells us, "The words of the wise are persuasive." In 1 Peter 3:15–16, we find we are to give the reason for the hope we have with gentleness and respect. Herein lies our working definition of persuasive pressure—words from wise parents spoken with gentleness and respect. In other words, the greatest hope we have in raising StrongHearts is to apply persuasive pressure with gentleness and respect. That doesn't mean being soft, but firm and fair.

Rev. John Lin, theologian-in-residence at the Harvard Law School, gives us a further understanding of persuasive pressure: "Where coercion forces agreement and compliance, persuasion seeks to recruit and partner."[10] Our countenance is the beginning of our persuasion. If we parent in our God-given place of authority over our children, we garner their respect. We invite our children to partner with us in their upbringing when they recognize we're not against them, but for them.

Let's examine the use of persuasive pressure that uses respect as the foundation for parenting and for building your family.

The Ruby Rule

Respect needs to be one of the nonnegotiables in your home. Respect should be expected. Disrespect should not be tolerated.

Where to start? Implement a twist on the Golden Rule as the cornerstone of your family's value system: "Respect others the way you want to be respected." The "Ruby Rule," as I like to call it, puts respect at the forefront of everyone's thinking.

When Mom respects Dad the way he wants to be respected and Dad respects Mom the way she wants to be respected, children receive lessons in respect that will establish a basis for their interactions with you. Oftentimes, the most powerful lessons your children learn are not the ones learned directly, but indirectly by observation.

Psychologist Jim Taylor reminds us, "If you teach your children to respect you, others and themselves when they are young, they're likely to carry that value with them as they enter the real world and use it to become successful and contributing adults."[11]

No other house rule brings peace to a home the way the "Ruby Rule" does! And it should be noted that no other rule of behavior will make up for the lack of respect in a home.

Respect for Others

You know upon entering someone's home whether respect is present or not, don't you? You hear it in the tone of voice used, you see it in how siblings interact with each other, and you feel it in the welcome you receive from family members.

How do we generate respect in our homes that is palpable to visitors? Consider these three critical components of building respect in your home:

1. *Respect each other and your children.* Knowing respect cannot be demanded, you must command respect by your love.

a. Love forgives quickly without condemnation.
b. Love excuses without fault.
c. Love speaks words of kindness rather than harshness.
d. Love commands respect.

2. *Do not allow children to show disrespect in actions or words to their siblings.* Have you ever broken up a fight between siblings? Two options:

a. How does it usually end? "Now, give your sister a hug," right? And there's still no better way to defuse unkind words and repair hurt feelings than a hug, especially if there is resistance, but it is carried out anyway.
b. Asking a child to clean the shoes of the other child teaches them how to:
   i. Walk in the other person's shoes, literally and figuratively
   ii. Respect the opinion of the other person
   iii. Be respectful of the feelings of their brother or sister

3. *Insist respect is shown to everyone who enters their home.*

   a. Putting down the cellphone or stopping the game when a guest arrives teaches children to show respect, which is putting the feelings of the guest ahead of their own interests in the moment.
   b. From the age of five, children should be expected to stand, speak, and shake the hand of the visitor with a word of welcome.

As these three basic guidelines for respect in your family become the underpinning of how you treat one another at home, they will become the gauge for how your children treat those beyond the four walls of your home.

Modeling Respect

Inconsistency in our words and actions not only breeds confusion, but disrespect. Children need to know we say what we mean, and we mean what we say. And they need to know we expect the same of ourselves that we expect of them. One of the most damaging things you can do to your children is to expect more of them than you do of yourself.

We all make mistakes, but we can minimize our mistakes in parenting when we are aware that who we are will greatly determine who our children become. When we are people of character and integrity, our children will respond with respect. Respect cannot be demanded; it is commanded by the way in which we live our lives. Do you remember Newton's Third Law?

> For every action, there is an equal and opposite reaction. The statement means that in every interaction, there is a pair of forces acting on the two interacting objects. The size of the force on the first object equals the size of the force on the second object. The direction of the force on the first object is opposite to the direction of the force

on the second object. Forces always come in pairs—equal and opposite action-reaction force pairs.[12]

Whatever action we take, our children will respond in kind:

- If you are habitually sassy with your five-year-old, she will return sass in her tone and posture.
- If you didn't treat your sixteen-year-old daughter with gentleness, kindness, and respect as a little girl, you can't expect her to be respectful of you.
- If you are rough with your children, they will pull away from you.
- If you are demanding and condescending to your fifteen-year-old son, he will not give you the time of day or have any interest in your advice.
- If you have no respect for authority, your twelve-year-old will have no respect for those in authority over him.
- If you scream at your children, they will scream louder.

Children don't calculate their actions the way adults do. They react to our actions and words by emulating our behavior. We cannot expect less of ourselves than we do of our children. They must see in us the same actions we expect in them:

- If we want our children to be forgiving, we must ask for forgiveness when we are disrespectful, neglectful, or forgetful.
- If we want our children to work hard, they must see a strong work ethic in us.
- If we want our children to be responsible with money, we must pay our bills on time, give generously to those in need, and spend within our means.

We must strive to be the people we want our children to become.

Littlest StrongHearts

My youngest granddaughters are five and six years old as of this writing. After spending the night at GG and Paw Paw's, the girls wanted to play school the next morning. The girls sat at the counter, while I played the role of teacher. It occurred to me this was a great opportunity to present the StrongHeart lesson to a kindergartener (Addison) and first grader (Elliott).

I drew the picture of StrongHeart on a whiteboard and asked the question, "What's in the heart of a StrongHeart?" Two hands excitedly reached for the sky.

"Addison, give me your answer first," I said.

"Love, it has to be love because love makes everybody's heart feel good," Addison replied, nodding her head up and down with great certainty.

"Absolutely correct, my girl," I answered, as I wrote LOVE in the center of the heart.

"Oh, I know another one, GG," Elliott shouted. "It's respecting."

I agreed, as I added the word RESPECT in StrongHeart's heart.

But Elliott was not satisfied. "No, GG, not respect. You have to put the 'ing' on the end because you have to be doing it, respecting others, not just talking about it!"

Wisdom far beyond her years.

We filled in StrongHeart's heart with other great attributes of the girls' choosing, until it was full.

When I asked the girls, "What will happen to StrongHeart's heart if he stops loving others?" Elliott grimaced as she replied, "Oh, GG, his heart will get dusty and hard to clean."

"Yeah, GG," added Addison. "His heart would get really dirty, and he wouldn't be able to live a good life."

Turns out, it's not only fifth graders we should listen to, but five- and six-year-olds too!

Parenting really does come down to this: it's not what's in your children's minds, but what's in their hearts that will determine who they become. The content of their hearts formulates the attitude that determines their actions. As fifth graders and tykes understand, what they think, say, and do originates in their hearts.

It's not what's in your children's minds, but what's in their hearts that will determine who they become.

Proverbs tells us, "For as he thinketh in his heart, so is he" (Prov. 23:7 KJV). That has been true since the beginning of time and will always be true. The world around us has changed dramatically in recent years, but your children's heart needs have not changed, and they will not change in the future.

If the content of your heart is truth and goodness, life still won't be perfect because it won't be without trials and disappointments. But it will be good, so good. You will be able to build solid relationships and raise good children who become great adults. You and your children will make a difference in your community and beyond.

Raising StrongHearts who . . .

Stand when others remain seated,

Speak while others remain silent,

Forgive when others refuse to forgive,

Lead in the right direction for others to follow,

And bow at the foot of the cross in worship and surrender to Christ. In bowing, our children will be empowered to stand strong. Do you know who raises a StrongHeart? Humble warriors, just like you, who prepare their children so they can become all God created them to be and carry out the great commission to share the good news.

Raising StrongHearts

A few years ago, my husband ordered firewood from a new group offering "good wood at a good price." Imagine our delight when young teenagers jumped out of the log truck to stack the firewood right where we wanted (the other side of the yard from the driveway), just as we wanted (stacked in our pipe stand behind the fireplace), and as high as we wanted. And to top it off, they did it with great attitudes, no complaints, no rolling eyes, and no cellphones.

When they completed the back-breaking work, they thanked us profusely for our business, shook my husband's hand with a robust shake, and asked us to tell our friends about their service. As they were leaving, one of the young men gave us a business card and said, "Remember Big Log Firewood next year." We did, and have, for the past five years.

But the backstory is really the better part of the story.

In 2014, six-year-old Henry was riding home from school with his dad when he asked for a four-wheeler. His dad responded by asking how he planned to pay for it. Henry said he wanted to start a business.

Since they had access to their grandparents' property, Henry thought selling firewood could help people (especially his grandparents, who cut and split their own wood) *and* make money. The original name for the business was Greene Log Firewood Specialties, since their last name is Greene, but when they were reminded that green logs aren't good for burning, they came up with Big Log. Even though big logs aren't the best for burning either, the name struck a "cord."

Henry's sisters went to work creating advertising fliers, knocking on doors, and soliciting business. Henry's dad enlisted help from his brother, Jason, for harvesting the wood. Henry's cousins jumped on board too.

The first year, Henry's dad loaded his pickup truck with wood and tried selling it with little success. Henry's parents and grandparents were the only customers.

Since these kids had been taught the importance of stick-to-itiveness, they didn't give up. The second year, they gained another customer and then another by knocking on doors and handing out business cards. As the years passed, Henry's sisters helped with sorting and loading wood and making deliveries.

Ten years later, Henry has become a sixteen-year-old with a payroll! Throughout the year, Henry and his hired help cut hundreds of face cords of firewood on Saturdays. In fact, this tenth grader and his buddies had split wood for seven hours the day before I interviewed the family on a Sunday afternoon.

Generations of StrongHearts

The Greene family has a long history of service and achievement. Henry's grandfather, a man of deep faith, is a veterinarian, rancher, engineer, and former state senator. He and his wife, Cathy, raised five children who are each making a difference in our world.

Even though Henry and his three sisters were born into an accomplished family, his parents make certain they understand that money can't trump the "glorious feeling of accomplishment"[13] and that adversity can build character.

Henry's dad, Boyd, shared the following comments during our interview:

> Resiliency is important. The word dictates that you will fail and must be able to come back from it. I allow my children to fail to build trust in our relationship. My only rule is respect with a good attitude. We're not helicopter parents. We're more like paratroopers, who "train up" our children for their mission in life. We prepare them for battle. Our oldest daughter will be dropped in the middle of the battle we call life on a college campus in just a few short months.

Meagan, Henry's mom, also grew up in a service-oriented home. Her dad worked long hours but made time to coach baseball and volunteer in the community. Her mom prepared hot meals for those less fortunate. It was important to Meagan's parents to pass on their values to their children.

Expressing her parenting concerns, Meagan said, "We don't want our children to cave to culture. We want them to have strength to fight the culture. We don't allow them to be lazy, because they would never find the ultimate joy in fulfilling their potential."

"We've tried to ground our children in truth, in the belief that the Word of God is true and perfect. The world doesn't know it, but it is true," Boyd interjected.

I asked the four Greene children, ages eleven to seventeen, their thoughts on lessons learned from their parents:

- "Their selflessness is amazing, always making sure our needs are met."
- "They taught us to think about how you can be a blessing to someone else. Do all you can for others. Put others before yourself all the time."
- "When they fail, they acknowledge it and admit they're wrong, so we can too."
- "Our parents don't tell us what we want to hear, but what we need to hear."

Ramsey Claire, Henry's seventeen-year-old sister who serves in areas of leadership at her school, said, "Selfishness spirals in one direction. Selflessness spirals in another direction. Either for better or worse."

Fourteen-year-old Madeleine added emphatically, "Everyone judges you for everything, so if you're going to be wrong, no matter what, be wrong on the right side. So, if I base my worth and identity in what others think of me, especially when they believe I'm wrong . . . I will always be disappointed."

No doubt, Meagan and Boyd Greene are raising another generation of StrongHearts!

Glorious Sense of Accomplishment

The glorious sense of accomplishment is a major theme in the Greene household. Boyd emphasized it over and over. This is what persuasive parenting is all about. Raising StrongHearts who will be able to stand up when others remain seated. Children who will speak up when others remain silent. Children who will lead in the right direction for others to follow. Children who will stand up for the right. Children who will stand against the wrong.

For your children's good and God's glory, do all you can to help your children reach their full potential to become who God created them to be. You will never know a greater sense of accomplishment than to see your children flourish. Your children will never know a greater joy than to feel God's pleasure in fulfilling the roles for which they were created.

◆ ◆ ◆

The truth is . . . identity is *the* question, isn't it? Always has been. Always will be. Our sacred honor and holy duty as parents is to help our children uncover their true identity from the Creator, like a gemologist unearthing a piece of rock that needs tumbling and chiseling to reveal the masterpiece of His design. Who they are and whose they are. To give them an unequivocal, indisputable, solid foundation on which they can stake their claim and build their lives. A foundation so firm that no matter what the world throws against them, they won't lose their footing. We know they *will* stumble, and they *may* fall, but they *will* get back up, sturdier than before as a true StrongHeart.

See, I set before you today life and prosperity
[*through the window of God's grace*],
death and destruction [*found in the mirror of man's race*].
For I command you today to love the LORD your God,
to walk in obedience to him,
and to keep his commands, decrees and laws;
then you will live and increase,
and the LORD your God will bless you
in the land you are entering to possess.
Now choose life [*through the window of God's grace*],
so that you and your children may live
and that you may love the LORD your God,
listen to his voice, and hold fast to him.
For the LORD is your life.

(Deut. 30:15–16; 19–20)

CONCLUSION

A Beloved StrongHeart

Beneath the gratitude, guts, respect, integrity, tenacity, humility, and resiliency of a StrongHeart lies a heart of love. Unselfish, unconditional love for our fellow man. The rare kind of love that is divinely human. Love that is patient and kind. Never jealous. Not boastful or proud. Love that esteems others rather than self. Even-tempered, forgives wrongs. Walks in truth. Filled with hope that never gives up.

The Backstory Determines the Front Story

In a book or movie, the backstory reveals important information about the main character's history that leads to the story you're reading about or watching. Former events in the character's life set in motion the outcome you're witnessing in the present chapter or on the screen.

"A character's backstory comprises all the data of his history, revealing how he became who he is, and why he acts as he does and thinks as he thinks."[1]

While there are many factors that play into how our children will navigate life as adults, the goals we set in raising them will help determine how hard or difficult it will be for them to find fulfillment in adulthood.

How true it is that *who* we become as adults is the result of our back-story as children.

Children who are well-loved, love well. Children who know they are loved unconditionally are free to love others without strings attached. These children collect more friends than trinkets. A heart that is filled to overflowing with love, God's love, loves freely. The spigot stays open, but the well never runs dry.

The Story of a StrongHeart

I knew a young woman who loved well, a beloved StrongHeart.

Laura Treppendahl was a selfless young woman who loved more deeply in nineteen years of life than most of us will love in seventy years of living. I agree with a dear friend of Laura's who said, "Laura lives out of an abundance of love," while most of us "live out of a hunger for it."[2]

Laura's college friend Ruthie Lindsey described Laura this way:

> She was absolutely beautiful, but she also had this kindness and ease about her. Every human that had the opportunity to be in her presence also felt it. . . . People were drawn to her and felt loved by her. . . . Laura had something figured out that I didn't have a clue about. People were drawn in because she made them feel so loved and accepted. She understood how loved and valued she was and out of that love she was able to freely love others.[3]

Laura never recognized her beauty, within or without. She was oblivious to the deep admiration of others. Not unlike other teenage girls, she wrestled with finding peace in her personhood during middle school and early high school. During the summer of 2000, just before her senior year, she was part of a work crew at the Great Escape—three weeks of intense leadership training for middle school students.

Daily devotionals were given to the work crew to help them grow in maturity while they worked with younger teens. The topic of identity was chosen for this group of teens (identity is *not* a new topic, nor does it have a new solution). The work crew members were asked to make a list of anything that identified them, nouns and adjectives, a fill-in-the-blank kind of exercise: I am ____________. Son, daughter, friend, football player, pianist, nerd, skinny, fat, short, tall, scared, tired, stupid, sad, etc.

"Some names build us up, others tear us down," explained their leader, Phyllis. "Some names describe things you participate in, such as sports and music. Some describe your attributes—patient, short-tempered, anxious. Others describe who you are, like brother, sister, grandchild. Some even describe who others say you are—stupid, ugly, loser. Some are true, some are not."

Phyllis's purpose was to direct this group of teen-leaders-in-the-making in a pursuit of truth. "While we are together for three weeks, I want to help you find how God sees you. His names for you. Reflect how He feels about you, your place in His family," Phyllis explained. She gave the teens a long list of God's names for His children, "God sees you as Blessed, His Chosen. He sees you as Forgiven, His Beloved. Adopted, His Heir."[4]

When Laura heard "Beloved," she beamed, exclaiming, "Yes, yes!" Laura embraced the concept of being beloved wholeheartedly. Of being dearly loved. Of being fully loved. Cherished. Precious. Sweet. Darling.

From this point forward, the parts of Laura's life that had been upside down, turned right side up. This kindhearted, faith-filled young girl became a courageous StrongHeart.

As a senior in high school, Laura was elated when her best friend was chosen for the homecoming court. Laura loved her dearly and was so proud of her and for her. When Laura's name was also announced, she was shocked and sat quietly in utter disbelief.

Just before the homecoming court made its way to the fifty-yard line on the night of the big game, Laura shared her excitement that she would be in a position to give her best friend the first congratulatory hug as the new queen. But Morgan's name was not called. It was Laura who was called forward to be honored. Laura burst into tears. Not tears of joy, but tears of disappointment that her dear friend was not crowned.

Accepting with grace, she acknowledged each member of the court as a queen.

Following graduation, Laura found her way to Ole Miss and into the hearts of her classmates and professors. In February of her sophomore year, a freshman slid behind the wheel of his Tahoe packed with eight buddies to head home from a Thursday night of bar hopping. Laura was headed home from her Bible study group. After sideswiping another vehicle, the young man hit Laura head on. She died on impact with hardly a scar on her body.

The following week, the sanctuary of First Presbyterian Church in Baton Rouge was standing room only with rows of those who loved Laura standing on the steps and spilled onto the sidewalks listening to the stories of this beautiful young woman's love-filled life.

Two weeks later, her boyfriend's roommate penned these moving words:

> She is the person in your life that smiles simply because she knows no other expression. She laughs because she finds that it soothes the soul, and it makes her smile even more. Her presence in a room brings great joy, yet comfort for the ones who do not have the social graces as others. She always exudes happiness when she sees you. It seems almost fake, but when you begin to see how she works, you understand that she truly is ecstatic to simply say "hello." When speaking with her, at that moment in time, you are the most important. She possessed the wonderful gift of listening. But more

importantly, she was compassionate when listening. If you were sad, she was sad; if you were hurting, she probably felt your pain; when you were excited, she elevated even more excitement. Her humbleness is perplexing, her willingness to serve others is convicting, and her ability to love others is gripping.[5]

Laura's life confirmed the life-transforming, life-sustaining attributes of a StrongHeart:

- She respected everyone, without notice of creed, race, or social status.
- She radiated joy as illuminating as a ray of sunlight on a fresh cut gemstone.
- She was generous with her love and grateful for every day to love more.
- She projected humble confidence in living to make others feel important.
- She lived without reserve with guts, resiliency, integrity, and tenacity.
- She exhibited moral courage as she braved the temptations of college life.
- She lived and loved in the window of God's grace.

Laura would have turned forty this year. Even after more than twenty years, the sweet aroma of Laura Treppendahl lingers among those privileged to have known her kindness, her love, and her hugs.

Yes, it *is* true . . . a child who is well-loved, loves well. The ultimate mark of a StrongHeart.

Appendix A

Calling All Dads

Our rapidly changing society makes the climate of our culture heavier and harder. According to a 2021 Gallup poll, "Americans are discouraged about the state of moral values in the U.S., with 84% calling them 'only fair' or 'poor' and two-thirds believing they are getting worse rather than better, evidenced by the escalation of sex, violence, and drug use."[1] The steep decline in moral values is a direct cause of the steep decline in all aspects of our culture.

If we agree we need to raise the moral standards of our culture, we must address two unpopular topics here as a place to start.

Profanity and Vulgar Language

The first difficult topic is profanity. People of every race and educational level use it. In surveys, six in ten people use strong language as part of their daily lives. About a third of people say they use strong language more than they did five years ago.[2] Research indicates the frequency gap between men and women is closing quickly. It's not just profanity that is heard in the public square, but vulgarity too. No subject is taboo. No words are unacceptable, but most parents still say they do not want their children using profanity or vulgarity. Really? Quite a disconnect here.

I could give a litany of statistics on the use of profanity and vulgar language on primetime shows, in the movies, on the airwaves, in print, and in the public square, but I won't. We all know how bad it is. Many of the same people who do not want to hear children swearing, swear themselves. Sounds a bit disrespectful of children, don't you think?

Believe it or not, there was a time, not that long ago, that a gentleman would call down another man for using rough language in front of his wife or daughter. Maybe that is the place to start . . . one word at a time.

Calling all dads, first and foremost!

My husband's father taught him and his three brothers all they needed to know about the use of profanity in a brave act of chivalry. One Saturday morning a neighbor was standing in the driveway visiting with a friend who was using profanity in a tone that could be heard well beyond the neighbor's house. Being a man who refused to use profanity (unless you consider his made-up word "dodvojit" used in moments of frustration a cuss word), he felt compelled to speak up.

"Pop" walked over to the neighbor with his friend and said, "Excuse me. My children and wife are in the yard. I do not appreciate this kind of language being used in front of my family." He returned to his yard without looking back. Neither of the men spoke another word as the visitor walked to his car to leave.

My husband said he learned in that moment to never allow anyone to show his wife or children disrespect in their actions or words.

Here's a question for you to ponder: What is it that makes us swallow words rather than spew them at certain times in certain places in front of certain people? It's respect, isn't it? Respect for the reverence of ceremonies or events, the sacredness of places of worship or learning, and most of all, respect for certain people . . . for who they are and what they represent.

You are the greatest influence of all in this area of manhood. If you don't use the choice language of the day, chances are great that your son won't use it either out of respect for you, others, and himself.

Cleaning up our trash talk is the first place to start in reversing our moral standards and expecting the same of our sons and daughters. Most importantly, standards befitting a new generation of StrongHearts.

Sexy or Pretty?

The second issue we must address is the fact that our oversexualized culture tells girls at every turn to be sexy not pretty. From singers to celebrities to magazines to even young women who don't know the difference. The message of our day is clear—what you look like on the outside is more important than who you are on the inside.

First and foremost . . . calling all dads!

The world doesn't tell girls that guys have a hard time seeing past the outside. The truth is, the sexy exterior is a poor reflection of what they really want and need, which is to be treated like a pretty lady.

Spend a Saturday at any major university during football season and you will see an ugly truth played out in front of you—girls who are desperate for attention dress provocatively to be seen, but the attention they crave is not the attention they get. Rather than being treasured, they are used and discarded. Remember our two precious sixteen-year-old girls from the first chapter? One made a wise decision rooted in humble confidence, and the other a poor decision rooted in misguided confidence.

How do you help your daughter choose the right path? Your daughter's perception of herself begins when she's a toddler. The way your daughter looks at herself is a reflection of how she is viewed by you, Dad.

If you want your daughter to cultivate her true identity in Christ, she needs to know you see her as precious in His sight. She needs to know she is cherished by you. She needs to know you will protect her innocence. She needs you to model the kind of man you want her to marry one day.

Beginning in elementary school, she needs to know you have high standards of dress and behavior befitting a lady. I know Mom is usually the one who deals with the clothing guidelines, but Dad, consider how you can encourage your daughter to present herself in a way that honors God, her family, and herself. In addition, how you respect her mother and how you view women will influence how your daughter sees herself.

You can give your daughter the strength she needs to hold her head high and start a new trend among her friends. She can be a leader who shows her generation the beauty of modesty and ladylike behavior befitting a StrongHeart.

Appendix B

The Purpose of Chores

As Roxanne, our mom of eight, shared in chapter 4, chores have been an important part of the training of her children with beautiful results. Her children, from youngest to oldest, are willing and able to help others. They find great satisfaction in serving without expectation of return.

Roxanne's oldest son is a gifted technology expert in the early stages of building his career. I hired him to do a video project for Manners of the Heart. When the project was completed, he said, "This one is on me. I'm glad I could be of service." The humble heart of a StrongHeart!

Ideally, you want to start young when kids are eager to help. We squelch their desire to help by not taking the time to help them learn *how* to help when they're young. I know it's easier to do it yourself, but we deprive our children of valuable lessons when we don't assign chores young enough.

Here are a few helpful suggestions for becoming a household that works together for the good of all:

- Set clear expectations. You can't be disappointed in your child's performance if you didn't take time to explain your expectation.

When my sons turned twelve, it was time they learned to cut the grass. One Saturday morning, I called the boys to the backyard. I put the gas can and lawnmower on the sidewalk and said, "Here you go, guys. Get after it!" After a half hour, they came barreling in the house, totally exasperated. "Mom, we're trying. But Mom, you can't just tell us to do it. You have to show us how to do it!" Ouch! Lesson learned!

- Appoint your children as directors of chores. Your oldest could be the Director of Maintenance (cleaning the car, vacuuming, mowing the yard). The youngest could be the Director of Trash. Give each of them routine, daily assignments in addition to their larger commitments.
- Give a combination of personal and family chores. Everyone should clean up after themselves (wet towels, clothes, school materials, etc.). Each child should also have chores that benefit the family (taking out the garbage, meal prep, yardwork, etc.).
- No nagging. Make the assignments and then wait and see. If the garbage isn't emptied, the trash will pile up. If the dishes aren't washed, there will be no plates to use. The child responsible will quickly feel the pressure from other family members to carry their load.
- With your youngest children, do the chore with them, until they're comfortable doing it on their own. Just don't do it for them, but with them.
- Chores can even be fun when there is a designated time for everyone to pitch in. You can play music and whistle while you work. (I know that was so corny!) Hey, maybe you could play "Flight of the Bumble Bee" to encourage children not to dawdle. Everyone can be reminded the sooner they get it done, the more time they'll have to play.

- Don't let your children off the hook when they ask to skip chores to do homework. Madeline Levine, author of *Teach Your Children Well*, says, "Being slack about chores when they compete with school sends your child the message that grades and achievement are more important than caring about others. What may seem like small messages in the moment, add up to big ones over time."[1]
- Here's the most important of all reminders: Don't jump in and "fix" the mistakes your children make when doing chores. Coming behind them to "perfect" their tasks removes their sense of pride in the job they've done and keeps your children from developing a sense of purpose in being valuable family members.

Family Armor Prayer

I encourage you to pray this prayer from Ephesians 6 every morning for your family. If you're single, use the singular pronouns. If married, use the singular/plural pronouns.

Lord, place upon my (our) head the helmet of salvation,
To protect my (our) mind.
Place upon my (our) chest the breastplate of righteousness,
To protect my (our) heart.
Buckle around me (us) the belt of Truth,
That I (we) would know the Truth and speak the Truth,
That I (we) would not be deceived, nor would I (we) deceive.
Lord, I (we) will carry the sword of the Spirit,
Your Word, as an offensive weapon.
Enable me (us) to walk in the path of peace
You lay before me (us) this day,
Not stepping to the left nor to the right but walking
in its narrow way.
With the Holy Spirit dwelling within,
With Jesus Christ, my (our) brother, standing with me (us),
And with the Lord God Almighty empowering me (us),

I (We) will hold the shield of faith this day
for [your children's / grandchildren's names]
Until each can carry it in their own faith,
knowing when the day is done,
We will still stand.
In Jesus' Name, Amen.

Resources

If you've found *StrongHeart* to be helpful in your parenting quest, I encourage you to visit jillgarnercontent.org/lessons for more inspiration and practical suggestions. You will find:

Lessons in humility	Lessons in integrity
Lessons in respect	Lessons in resilience
Lessons in gratitude	Lessons in self-respect
Lessons in tenacity	Lessons in building a strong home

To access a small group study guide, including discussion questions and HeartWork for the Home, visit jillgarnercontent.org/smallgroupstudy.

To deepen your knowledge of the principles of raising a StrongHeart, find movie guides with discussion questions for your family at jillgarner content.org/movies.

To broaden your understanding of the application of the principles, find book recommendations with discussion questions for personal study at jillgarnercontent.org/books.

To help your children understand and apply the lessons of *StrongHeart*, visit jillgarnercontent.org/books for a list of children's books divided by age group and topic with discussion questions for engagement with your child.

To find a detailed description of the generations, as outlined in the book, visit jillgarnercontent.org/generations.

To bring *HeartEd* into your home or your children's school, visit manners oftheheart.org for more information about our curricula and training for homeschool, Christian schools, and public schools.

Acknowledgments

To my ever-patient husband, Nick, the man who has never once said "Not now" to my question, "Can I read you something?" I love you more today than yesterday.

To my sons, Boyce and Chad, who have endured the retelling of "their" stories over and over and over again.

To my daughter-in-law, Elise, who loves my son and youngest granddaughters with all her heart.

To our children, Robert and Mary, Rich and Sally, Burton and Lea, thank you for loving me.

To my seven grandchildren who call GG when they need a hug. I love you more.

To Donna, my big sister in Christ, who continues to walk alongside me with prayer and wise counsel.

To the ladies of Manners of the Heart, Shelly, Pam, Anita, Anna, Sarah, and Myrna, who endure countless meetings and boring soliloquies as I sift through the ramblings in my heart to find His guidance. Manners of the Heart wouldn't be without you.

To the multitude of families who shared their stories of triumph and defeat, mistakes and successes. You know who you are and Whose you are. Thank you for allowing me the privilege of sharing your wisdom for the benefit of other parents.

To the Manners of the Heart board members, parents, teachers, volunteers, and donors who share my passion and support our efforts to raise a generation of StrongHearts.

To the up-and-coming young StrongHearts who are following Wise Ol' Wilbur's teachings.

To Steve Laube who gave an immediate yes when asked if he would step back in.

To Judy Dunagan for her understanding and kind heart in the acquisitions process.

To the Moody Publishers team, especially Amanda Cleary Eastep, who shared their expertise in the production process from editing to marketing.

To the One who called me to this work and makes it all possible. It is for the sake of the children of the next generation and for His glory alone.

Notes

CHAPTER ONE: Choose Self-Respect, Forget Self-Esteem

1. "Strong," *Webster's Dictionary 1828*, https://webstersdictionary1828.com/Dictionary/strong.
2. Nathaniel Branden, *The Psychology of Self-Esteem* (New York: Bantam, 1969), Introduction.
3. Frank Stephenson, "For the Love of Me," Florida State University Research in Review, Summer 2004, https://homepages.se.edu/cvonbergen/files/2013/01/For-the-Love-of-ME.pdf.
4. *The Journal of Ayn Rand Studies*, Penn State University Press, December 2016, https://www.jstor.org/stable/10.5325/jaynrandstud.16.1-2.issue-1-2.
5. Danielle Guth, "Self-Esteem and Mental Health," February 19, 2023, https://suburbanresearch.com/2023/02/19/self-esteem-and-mental-health/.
6. Ibid.
7. J. Bosson and W. B. Swann Jr., "Self-Esteem: Nature, Origins, and Consequences," in R. Hoyle & M. Leary, eds., *Handbook of Individual Differences in Social Behavior* (New York: Guilford, 2009), 527–46.
8. J. Walker (Producer) and B. Bird (Director), *Incredibles* [Motion Picture]. United States: Disney/Pixar, 2004.
9. "Chanak," https://www.bibletools.org/index.cfm/fuseaction/Lexicon.show/ID/H2596/chanak.htm.
10. "Derek," https://kingjamesbibledictionary.com/StrongsNo/H1870/way.
11. Committee Opinion, "Mental Health Disorders in Adolescents," American College of Obstetrics and Gynecology, https://www.acog.org/clinical/clinical-

guidance/committee-opinion/articles/2017/07/mental-health-disorders-in-adolescents.

12. Lea Winerman, "By the Numbers: Antidepressant Use Is on the Rise," American Psychological Association, November 2017, https://www.apa.org/monitor/2017/11/numbers.
13. Committee Opinion, "Mental Health Disorders in Adolescents," American College of Obstetrics and Gynecology, https://www.acog.org/clinical/clinical-guidance/committee-opinion/articles/2017/07/mental-health-disorders-in-adolescents.
14. Ibid.
15. American College Health Association. American College Health Association-National College Health Assessment III: Undergraduate Student Reference Group Executive Summary, Spring 2022. Silver Spring, MD: American College Health Association, Spring 2022.
16. Ibid.
17. Ibid.
18. Jennifer Crocker, "The Cost of Seeking Self-Esteem," *Journal of Social Issues*, December 17, 2002, https://doi.org/10.111/1540-4569.00279.
19. David Brooks, *The Road to Character* (New York: Random House, 2016), 14.
20. "Your Toddler's Possessive Phase, Explained," Hendersonville Pediatrics, PA, https://www.hendersonvillepediatrics.com/blog/89-your-toddler-s-possessive-phase-explained.html.
21. J. A. Armour and J. Ardell, eds., *Neurocardiology* (New York: Oxford University Press, 1994).
22. M. Guarneri, *The Heart Speaks* (New York: Atria, 2019), 156.
23. Elisabeth Elliot, "The Vice of Self-Esteem," September/October 1999, https://elisabethelliot.org/resource-library/newsletters/the-vice-of-self-esteem-2/.

CHAPTER TWO: Establish the Home of Respect

1. "Strong," https://kingjamesbibledictionary.com/Dictionary/strong.
2. Arianna, "What is a Biblical Worldview and Why Is It Important in Education?" Homeschool Blog from bjupress, July 27, 2021, https://blog.bjupress.com/blog/2021/07/27/biblical-worldview-in-education/.
3. Alison J. Gray, "Worldviews," *Int. Psychiatry* 8(3) (August 2011): 58–60. PMID: 31508085; PMCID: PMC6735033. National Library of Medicine, https://www.ncbi.nlm.nih.gov/pmc/articles/PMC6735033/.

4. George Barna, "Does My Child's Worldview Really Matter?" May 18, 2015, https://godlyparent.com/does-worldview-really-matter.
5. Ibid.
6. Jill Rigby, *Raising Respectful Children in a Disrespectful World* (Enumclaw, WA: Redemption Press, 2023).
7. Bret Eckleberry, "Honor Your Father and Your Mother," Focus on the Family, July 21, 2023, https://www.focusonthefamily.com/live-it-post/honor-your-father-and-mother/.
8. George Barna, "Research Shows That Spiritual Maturity Process Should Start at a Young Age," https://www.barna.com/research/research-shows-that-spiritual-maturity-process-should-start-at-a-young-age/.
9. Jeff Diamant, Elizabeth Sciupac, "10 Key Findings about the Religious Lives of US Teens and Their Parents," Pew Research Center, September 10, 2020, https://www.pewresearch.org/short-reads/2020/09/10/10-key-findings-about-the-religious-lives-of-u-s-teens-and-their-parents/.
10. "The Harmful Effects of Excessive Screentime for Kids," The Pragmatic Parent, https://www.thepragmaticparent.com/harmful-effects-of-too-much-screen-time-for-kids/.

CHAPTER THREE: Replace Happiness with Joy

1. "Strong," https://kingjamesbibledictionary.com/Dictionary/strong.
2. Christopher Curley, "Survey Details What Parents Want Most for Their Children," Healthline, January 24, 2023. https://www.healthline.com/health-news/mental-health-financial-stability-among-parents-top-hopes-for-their-children#Reaction-from-experts-to-parents-survey
3. "Suicide," National Institute for Mental Health, https://www.nimh.nih.gov/health/statistics/suicide.
4. "The State of Mental Health in America," Mental Health America, 2023 Statistics, https://mhanational.org/issues/state-mental-health-america.
5. Denise Stack, "Managing Anxiety in the Classroom," December 11, 2016. https://mhanational.org/blog/managing-anxiety-classroom.
6. "Social Anxiety Disorder," Mental Health America, https://mhanational.org/conditions/social-anxiety-disorder.
7. "Data and Statistics on Children's Mental Health," https://www.cdc.gov/childrensmentalhealth/data.html.

8. John Rosemond, Facebook post, August 3, 2023, https://www.facebook.com/johnkrosemond.
9. Alice George, "The Teddy Bear Was Once Seen as a Dangerous Influence on Young Children," *Smithsonian Magazine*, December 2023, https://www.smithsonianmag.com/history/history-teddy-bear-once-seen-dangerous-influence-young-children-180983234/.
10. Walt Disney, "The Mainstreet Mouse," https://www.themainstreetmouse.com/2012/12/15/good-can-always-triumph-over-evil-walt-disney/.
11. Gary Cross, *The Cute and the Cool: Wondrous Innocence and Modern American Children's Culture* (Oxford University Press, 2004).
12. "Data and Statistics on Children's Mental Health," https://www.cdc.gov/childrensmentalhealth/data.html.
13. "Treat," The Oxford Pocket Dictionary of Current English, https://www.encyclopedia.com/humanities/dictionaries-thesauruses-pictures-and-press-releases/treat-0. Emphasis added.
14. "Treat," *Merriam-Webster*, 2023, https://www.merriam-webster.com/dictionary/treat (italics mine).
15. Peter Susic, "45+ Video Game Addiction Statistics (2023): How Many People Are Addicted?" Headphones Addicts, July 5, 2023, https://headphonesaddict.com/video-game-addiction/.
16. Video Game Addiction, https://www.video-game-addiction.org/video-game-addiction-articles/top-10-alternatives-to-video-games-04381.htm.
17. Katie Ely, "Unstructured Play: Why Kids Need It," Parenting with Focus, February 24, 2021, https://www.parentingwithfocus.org/post/why-your-child-needs-1-2-hours-of-independent-unstructured-play-every-day.
18. Michael Yogman et al., "The Power of Play: A Pediatric Role in Enhancing Development in Young Children," *Pediatrics* 142, no. 3 (September 2018), https://doi.org/10.1542/peds.2018-2058.
19. Art Linkletter, *Kids Say the Darndest Things!*" (Englewood Cliffs, NJ: Prentice-Hill, Inc., 1957), 113.
20. Matthew McConaughey, "University of Houston Speech 720p," YouTube, May 23, 2018, video, https://www.youtube.com/watch?v=3QWQKrJkR9A.
21. Judith Tedlie Moskowitz, "Good Feelings in the Midst of Chronic Pain," *Scientific American*, January 4, 2018, https://blogs.scientificamerican.com/observations/good-feelings-in-the-midst-of-chronic-pain/.

CHAPTER FOUR: Instill a Heart of Gratitude

1. "Strong," King James Bible Dictionary, https://kingjamesbibledictionary.com/Dictionary/strong.
2. Gary Sernovitz, "How to Hitch a Ride on a Mardi Gras Float," *Wall Street Journal*, July 17, 2019, https://www.wsj.com/articles/how-to-hitch-a-ride-on-a-mardi-gras-float-11551370431.
3. "Trinket," *Merriam-Webster*, 2023, merriam-webster.com.
4. "Treat," *Merriam-Webster*, 2023, merriam-webster.com.
5. Jill Garner, *HeartED*, Baton Rouge, LA: Manners of the Heart, 2022.
6. Jill Rigby, *Raising Unselfish Children in a Self-Absorbed World* (New York: Simon and Schuster, 2006), 191–92.
7. Personal interview/conversation, Roxanne Struppeck, May 2023.
8. Kelly Butler, "Mississippi Miracle," presentation to the Rotary Club of Baton Rouge, February 7, 2024.
9. "Chores and Children," American Academy of Adolescence, June 2018, https://www.aacap.org/AACAP/Families_and_Youth/Facts_for_Families/FFF-Guide/Chores_and_Children-125.aspx.
10. Marcus Dickinson, "The Entitled Generation: How Societal Shifts Have Changed Perspectives on Work," August 6, 2023, https://www.linkedin.com/pulse/entitled-generation-how-societal-shifts-have-changed-work-dickinson/.
11. Jennifer Wallace, "Why Children Need Chores," *The Wall Street Journal*, March 13, 2015, https://www.wsj.com/articles/why-children-need-chores-1426262655.
12. Elizabeth M. White, Mark D. DeBoer, and Rebecca J. Scharf, "Associations Between Household Chores and Childhood Self-Competency," *Journal of Developmental Behavioral Pediatrics* 40, no. 3 (April 2019): 176–82, doi: 10.1097/DBP.0000000000000637.
13. "Your Toddler's Possessive Phase, Explained," https://www.hendersonvillepediatrics.com/blog/89-your-toddler-s-possessive-phase-explained.html.
14. Ibid.
15. Good Samaritan, testimonial series, https://goodsamjc.org/testimonial-series.

CHAPTER FIVE: Foster Humility and Confidence

1. "Strong," https://www.powerthesaurus.org/strong/definitions.
2. Mother Teresa, https://www.vaticansite.com/st-mother-teresa-quotes-humility/.

3. "Humbleness," *Oxford Language*, https://www.google.com/search?q= definition+of+humility&oq.
4. "Humility," *Merriam-Webster's Dictionary*, https://www.merriamwebster .com/dictionary/humble.
5. Jonathan Sacks, "Humility," Covenant & Conversation, https://rabbisacks .org/covenant-conversation/behaalotecha/humility/.
6. Dave Adamson, "Anavah," July 19, 2019, https://radicalmentoring.com/ anavah/.
7. Dave Adamson, *52 Hebrew Words Every Christian Should Know* (Bloomington, IL: Christian Art Gifts), 43.
8. "The Big Picture: The Meaning of Life: Philosophers, Pundits and Plain Folk Ponder What It's All About," *Life Magazine*, Chicago, IL: Time, Inc., December 1988, 89.
9. Kerry Flatly, "Why Kids Need Chores to Be Successful in Life," Self-sufficient Kids, https://selfsufficientkids.com/how-chores-set-kids-up-success-life/.
10. Rabbi Jonathan Sacks, "Humility," Covenant & Conversation, https://www .rabbisacks.org/covenant-conversation/behaalotecha/humility/.
11. Personal conversation with a mom of two children, ages 10 and 14, August 2023.
12. Danny Huerta, "Teaching Kids How To Be Humble," Focus on the Family, https://www.focusonthefamily.com/parenting/teaching-kids-how-to-be-humble/.

CHAPTER SIX: Encourage Bravery

1. "Strong," *KJV Dictionary*, https://av1611.com/kjbp/kjv-dictionary/ strong.html.
2. Dr. George Barna, "Americans Are Most Likely to Base Truth on Feelings," February 12, 2002, https://www.barna.com/research/americans-are-most-likely-to-base-truth-on-feelings/.
3. Ibid.
4. George Barna, "American Worldview Inventory 2020, Arizona Christian University, May 19, 2020, https://www.arizonachristian.edu/wp-content/ uploads/2020/05/AWVI-2020-Release-05-Perceptions-of-Truth.pdf.
5. Ibid.
6. Jill Rigby, *Raising Respectful Children in a Disrespectful World* (Enumclaw, WA: Redemption Press, 2023).

7. Max Lucado, *I'm Not a Scaredy Cat* (Nashville, TN: Thomas Nelson), 2017.
8. Michelle Adams and Eva Marie Everson, *Our God Is Bigger Than That* (Nesbit, MS: End Game Press, 2022).
9. Lysa TerKeurst, *It Will Be Okay* (Nashville, TN: Thomas Nelson, 2014).
10. Interview with Boyd Greene, May 7, 2023.
11. Harper Lee, *To Kill a Mockingbird* (Philadelphia, PA: Warner Books, 1982), 112.
12. "Courage," Online Etymology Dictionary, https://www.etymonline.com/word/courage.
13. "Courage," https://www.dictionary.com/browse/courage.
14. "Courage," https://onelook.com/thesaurus/?s=courage.
15. Ibid.
16. Jason and Andrea Stern, personal interview, January 2023.
17. Vidor, King, et al. *The Wizard of Oz*. Metro-Goldwyn-Mayer (MGM), 1939.
18. Mark Twain, *Century Magazine*, Volume 47, Number 5, "Pudd'nhead Wilson," March 1894.

CHAPTER SEVEN: Develop GRIT (Guts, Resilience, Integrity, Tenacity)

1. "Strong," King James Bible Dictionary, https://kingjamesbibledictionary.com/Dictionary/stouthearted.
2. Angela Lee Duckworth, "Grit: The Power of Passion and Perseverance," TedTalk, April 2013, https://www.ted.com/talks/angela_lee_duckworth_grit_the_power_of_passion_and_perseverance/transcript.
3. John Bloom, "True Grit," DesiringGod.org, August 15, 2014, https://www.desiringgod.org/articles/true-grit.
4. Benjamin Franklin, https://www.quotes.net/quote/3873.
5. Ciara Byrne, "Generation Tech: More Kids Can Play Computer Games Than Ride a Bike," VentureBeat, January 19, 2011, https://venturebeat.com/games/kids-technology/.
6. "Resilience," Oxford Languages, https://www.google.com/search?q=resilience+definition.
7. "1970's Weebles Commercial," November 23, 2012, https://www.youtube.com/watch?v=dFzhjnjXc2o.
8. "Learning from Mistakes: Why We Need to Let Children Fail," Bright Horizons, July 15, 2021, https://www.brighthorizons.com/resources/Article/the-importance-of-mistakes-helping-children-learn-from-failure.

9. Henry Cloud, *Integrity: The Courage to Meet the Demands of Reality* (New York: HarperCollins, 2006).
10. Ibid., 85.
11. Michele Borba, "Seven Ways to Build Strong Character and Integrity in Children," http://micheleborba.com/blog/seven-tips-to-build-strong-character-and-help-kids-stand-up-for-their-moral-beliefs/.
12. "Tenacity," Vocabulary.com, August 10, 2022, https://www.vocabulary.com/dictionary/tenacity.
13. Sally Sigan, "8 Ways to Boost Memorization Skills," December 13, 2013, https://kidsdiscover.com/teacherresources/8-ways-to-boost-memorization-skills/.
14. Elizabeth Keller, "Get Your Students to Think Like an Innovator," April 24, 2023, https://kidsdiscover.com/teacherresources/students-to-think-like-an-innovator/.
15. Irene Howat, *Lightkeepers* (Ashland, OH: CF4Kids, 2009).
16. Erica R. Hendry, "7 Epic Fails Brought to You By the Genuis Mind of Thomas Edison," November 20, 2013, https://www.smithsonianmag.com/innovation/7-epic-fails-brought-to-you-by-the-genius-mind-of-thomas-edison-180947786/.
17. Poster for Thomas A. Edison 50th anniversary 1847–1997, United States Department of the Interior, National Park Service, Edison National Historic Site, West Orange, New Jersey, https://www.loc.gov/collections/edison-company-motion-pictures-and-sound-recordings/article-and-essays/biography/life-of-thomas-alva-edison-#note2.
18. Thomas Edison, https://www.thomasedison.org/edison-quotes.

CHAPTER EIGHT: Practice Others-Centeredness

1. "Strong," *Webster's Dictionary 1828,* https://webstersdictionary1828.com/Dictionary/strong.
2. Henry Cloud, *Integrity: The Courage to Meet the Demands of Reality* (New York: HarperCollins, 2006).
3. Clarence W. Stephens, "30 Stories of the Kindness of Strangers That Will Make You Tear Up," *Reader's Digest*, September 3, 2023, https://www.rd.com/article/kindness-strangers/.
4. "Empathy," *Webster's*, https://www.merriam-webster.com/dictionary/empathy.

5. Caroline Kee, "I'm a Pediatrician and Dad. Here's My No. 1 Tip to Raise Happy, Successful Kids," TODAY, July 5, 2023, https://news.yahoo.com/im-pediatrician-dad-heres-no-182101264.html.
6. Jordan Scott, "How Does a Mirror Work?" February 18, 2022, https://info.glass.com/how-does-a-mirror-work/.
7. Ibid.
8. Staff, "Gen Z Is the Loneliest Generation," *Relevant*, December 19, 2022, https://relevantmagazine.com/life5/gen-z-is-the-loneliest-generation/.
9. Jill Rigby, *Raising Unselfish Children in a Self-Absorbed World* (New York: Simon & Schuster, 2006).
10. Phil. 2: 3–4, Author's adaptation from the New International Version.

CHAPTER NINE: Champion Respect

1. "Strong," *King James Bible Dictionary*, https://kingjamesbibledictionary.com/Dictionary/stouthearted.
2. Nathan Maranto, clinical therapist, personal conversation, October 1, 2023.
3. Ibid.
4. Lindy and Dale Weiner, personal interview, March 2023.
5. Jill Rigby, *Raising Respectful Children in a Disrespectful World* (Enumclaw, WA: Redemption Press, 2023), 37.
6. Jill Rigby, *Raising Unselfish Children in a Self-Absorbed World* (New York: Simon & Schuster, 2006), 73.
7. "Fun Facts About Rubies," American Gem Society, July 12, 2021, https://www.americangemsociety.org/ruby-fun-facts.
8. MAT, Mahmut, "Ruby," April 4, 2023, https://geologyscience.com/gemstone/ruby/.
9. "Ruby History and Lore," GIA, https://www.gia.edu/ruby-history-lore.
10. Rev. John C. Lin, "Persuasion with Gentleness and Respect," March 7, 2022, https://pblcls.law.harvard.edu/blog/persuasion-with-gentleness-and-respect/.
11. Jim Taylor, "Parenting: Respect Starts at Home," *Psychology Today*, January 4, 2010, https://www.psychologytoday.com/us/blog/the-power-prime/201001/parenting-respect-starts-home.
12. Newton's Third Law," Newton's Laws-Lesson 4-Newton's Third Law of Motion, The Physics Classroom, https://www.physicsclassroom.com/class/newtlaws/Lesson-4/Newton-s-Third-Law.

13. Alex Leary, "This Is Bill the Other Koch Brother," *Tampa Bay Times*, November 2, 2014, https://www.tampabay.com/archive/2014/11/02/this-is-bill-the-other-koch-brother/.

CONCLUSION: A Beloved StrongHeart

1. Jessica Morrell, "What Backstory Can Do For Your Story," Writer's Digest University, August 21, 2008, https://www.writersdigest.com/qp7-migration-writers-digest-conference/between-the-lines-excerpt.
2. Ruthie Lindsey, *There I Am: The Journey from Hopelessness to Healing—A Memoir* (New York: Gallery Books, 2020), 57.
3. Ruthie Lindsey, February 7, 2019, https://www.facebook.com/ruthielindsey speaker/photos/a.263099024136774/601783906934949.
4. Phyllis Alexander, personal conversation, September 2023.
5. Johnathan Keenan, February 2003, http://onlylowercase.blogspot.com/2009/02/laura-treppendahl.html.

APPENDIX A

1. Linda Saad, "Stable US Moral Ratings Obscure Big Partisan Shifts," GALLUP, June 16, 2021, https://news.gallup.com/poll/351140/stable-moral-ratings-obscure-big-partisan-shifts.aspx.
2. Mark Brown, "Swearing on Rise, But Most Parents Still Don't Want Kids Hearing It, Report Finds," *The Guardian*, June 10, 2021, https://www.theguardian.com/science/2021/jun/10/swearing-on-rise-but-parents-still-dont-want-kids-hearing-it-report-finds.

APPENDIX B

1. Adrianne Fawcett, "Madeleine Levine: Chores Trump Homework," *Daily Northshore News*, March 23, 2011, https://jwcdaily.com/2011/03/23/madeline-levine-chores-trump-homework/.

MANNERS OF THE HEART

UNLOCKING THE HEART TO OPEN THE MIND

The mission of Manners of the Heart is to reawaken respect in our society for the sake of the next generation.

Manners of the Heart equips parents and educators with the tools to address the heart needs of children; teaching children to treat others the way their hearts want to be treated. Children's hearts are unlocked and their minds opened, so learning can begin.
We call this Heart Education.

WISE OL' WILBUR OF MERRYVILLE LIVES IN THE ONE AND ONLY HAPPLE TREE

AN ATTITUDE OF THE HEART

Manners of the Heart defines manners not as etiquette, but as an attitude of the heart that is **self-giving rather than self-serving**. Recent research is catching up to Scripture's teaching that the esteeming of God and others, rather than the esteeming of self, is where self-worth is ultimately found.

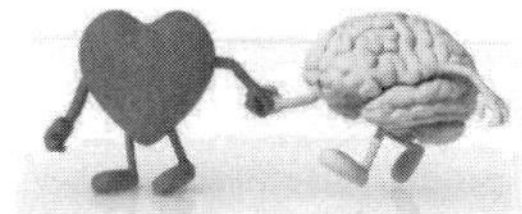

RESPECT-BASED HEART EDUCATION

Through our Heart Education curriculum, we support the heart-mind connection essential to developing the moral wisdom of children. **Love, Patience, Humility, Responsibility, Respect,** and **Self-Control** - these are just a few of the Heart Attributes our lessons instill.

STUDENTS LEARN 35 HEART ATTRIBUTES OVER THE COURSE OF THE SCHOOL YEAR.

RESPECT IN ACTION

As **children learn to respect and esteem others**, they gain respect for themselves. Self-respect translates into motivated, self-disciplined children with a desire to learn and a longing to become all they were created to be. These values instilled in the early years become the foundation for moral behavior in later years.

BUILDING STRONGHEARTS

Through Heart Education, we can build a generation of **StrongHearts: morally courageous kids with the head knowledge to lead and the heart knowledge to lead in the right direction.**